PIANO • VOCAL • GUITAR

THE COMPLETE BEATLES

VOLUME TWO

ARRANGED BY TODD LOWRY

7777 W. BLUEMOUND RD. P.O. BOX 13819 MILWAUKEE, WI 53213

CONTENTS

VOL

2

IT WON'T BE LONG

Words and Music by
PAUL McCARTNEY

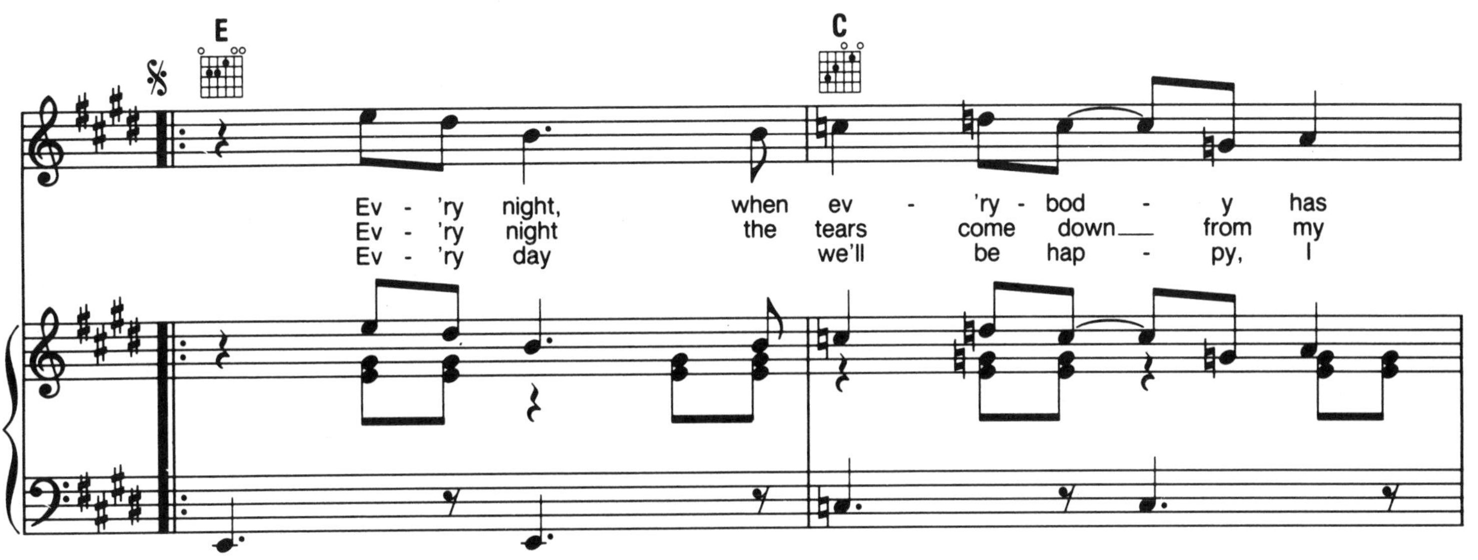
E
C
Ev - 'ry night, when ev - 'ry - bod - y has
Ev - 'ry night the tears come down from my
Ev - 'ry day we'll be hap - py, I

E
C
fun, Here am I sit - ting all on my
eyes, Ev - 'ry day I've done noth - ing but
know. Now I know that you won't leave me no

E
own.
cry.
more.
It won't be

C♯m
long yeah, (Yeah) yeah, (Yeah) yeah, (Yeah) It won't be
E
long yeah, (Yeah) yeah, (Yeah) yeah. (Yeah) It won't be
C♯m
To Coda
A
A♯dim
E
long yeah, (Yeah) till I be - long to you.
D♯+
Since you left me I'm so a - lone. now you're

Bm6/D
C#7
com - ing, you're com - ing on home.
A
B7
I'll be good like I know I should, You're com - ing
F#7
1 B7
2 B7
D.S. al Coda
home, you're com - ing home. home. So
3
CODA
A
G
F#
F
Emaj7
Slowly
I be - long to you.
rit.

IT'S ALL TOO MUCH

Words and Music by
GEORGE HARRISON

G
When I look in - to your eyes, your love is there for me.
Float - ing down the stream of time, from life to life with me.
Sail me on a sil - ver sun, where I know that I'm free

And the more I go in - side, the
Makes no dif - f'rence where you are, or
Show me that I'm ev - 'ry - where, and

C/G
G
more there is to see. It's all too much for
where you'd like to be. It's all too much for
get me home for tea. It's all too much for

Dsus/G
G
C/G
G
me to take, the love that's shin - ing all a -
me to take, the love that's shin - ing all a -
me to see, the love that's shin - ing all a -

C/G
G
Dsus/G
G
round you. Ev - 'ry - where, it's what you make, for
round here. All the world is birth - day cake, so
round here. The more I have, the less I know, and

C/G
G
To Coda
1
us to take, it's all too much
take a piece, but not too
what I do is all too

2
G
C/G
G
C6/G
G
much.
C/G
G
C/G
G
C6/G
G
C6/G
G
3
3
3
C/G
G
C6/G
G
C/G
G
C6/G

1
G
2
G
D.S. al Coda
CODA
G
C/G
G
Dsus/G
G
much. It's all too much_ for me to take,_ the
C/G
G
C/G
G
love that's shin - ing all a - round you. Ev - 'ry - where_ it's
Dsus/G
G
C/G
G
what you make,_ for us to take,_ it's all too much.

C/G
G
C/G
G
C/G
G
C6/G
It's too much.
G
C/G
G
C/G
G
Ah.
It's too much.
C/G
G
C6/G
G
tr
3

C/G
G
With your long blonde hair and your eyes of blue.
With your long blonde hair and your eyes of blue.

C/G
G
C/G
G
C/G
You're too much!
G
C/G
G
C/G
G
C6/G
G
Repeating and disintegrating
C/G
G
C
G
Too much!

JULIA

Words and Music by
JOHN LENNON and PAUL McCARTNEY

Am
Am7
B7
Ju - li - a,
sea - shell eyes,
sleep - ing sand,
o - cean
wind - y
si - lent

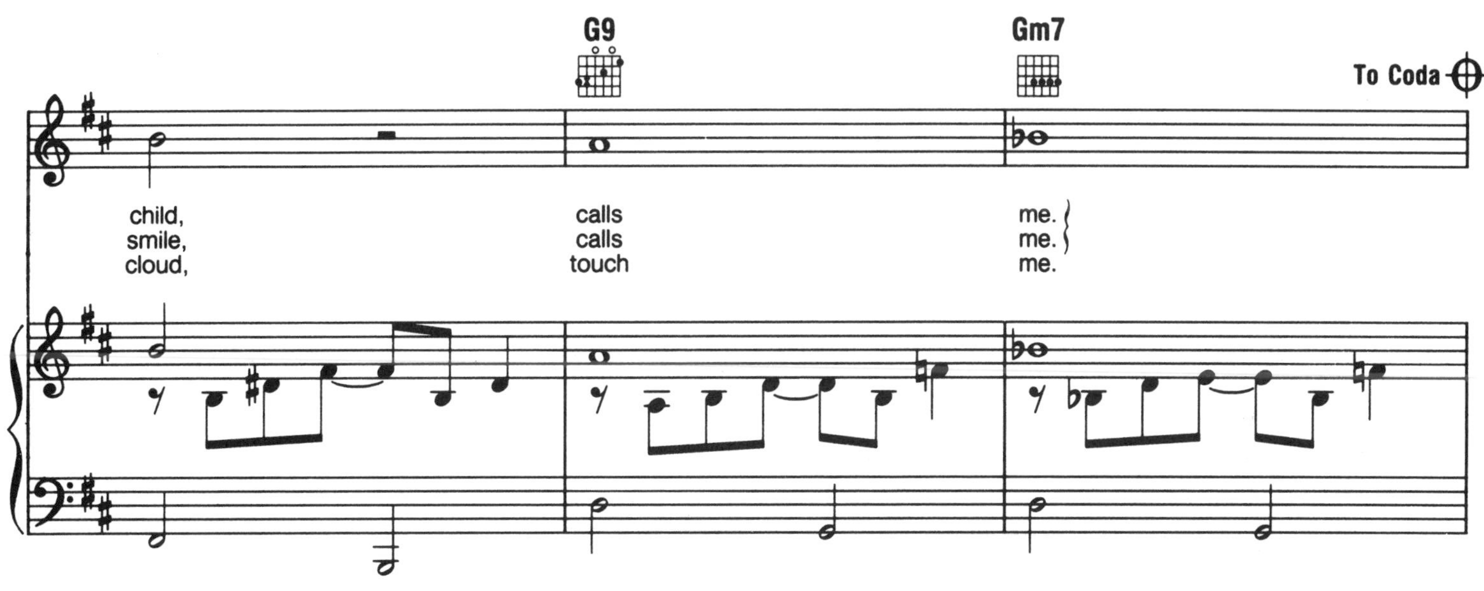
G9
Gm7
To Coda
child,
smile,
cloud,
calls
calls
touch
me.
me.
me.

D
Bm7
F#m
A
So I sing a song of love,
Ju - li -

D
C♯m
a.
Her hair of
D
float - ing sky is shim - mer - ing,
Bm7
Bm6
glim - mer - ing,
F♯m(add2)
F♯m6
F♯m(addD)
in the sun.

F♯m
D
Bm7
Ju - li - a.
Am
Am7
B7
Ju - li - a,
morn - ing
G9
Gm7
moon
touch
me.
D
Bm7
F♯m
So I sing a song of love,
Ju -

A
D
D.C. al Coda
- li - a.
CODA
D
Bm9
F♯m
So I sing a song of love, Ju -
A
D
Bm7
- li - a.
Am
Am7
B7
Mmm

G9
Gm7
calls
me.
D
Bm7
A
So I sing a song of love for Ju - li -
D
A
D
a. Ju - li - a,
F♯m
A
Dmaj7
Ju - li - a.

KANSAS CITY

Words and Music by JERRY LEIBER
and MIKE STOLLER

C7 F/C C7 G7 C/G G7 C/G

Gon - na get my ba - by back home, a yeah, yeah,
Gon - na get my ba - by one time, a yeah, yeah,

G7 C/G G7 D7 G/D D7

Well it's a long, long time since
It's just a one, two, three, four,

C7 F/C C7 G7 C/G G7 C/G

my ba - by's been gone.
five, six, sev - en, eight, nine.

1 G C7 C#7 D7 | 2 G C7 C#7 D7

Ah, Wow!

G7
C/G
G7
C/G
G7
C/G
G7
C/G
G7
C/G
G7
C/G
G7
C/G
G7
C7
F/C
C7
F/C
C7
F/C
C7
G7
C/G
G7
C/G
G7
C/G
G7
D7
G/D
D7
C7
F/C
C7
G7
C/G
G7
C/G
G

IT'S ONLY LOVE

Words and Music by
JOHN LENNON and PAUL McCARTNEY

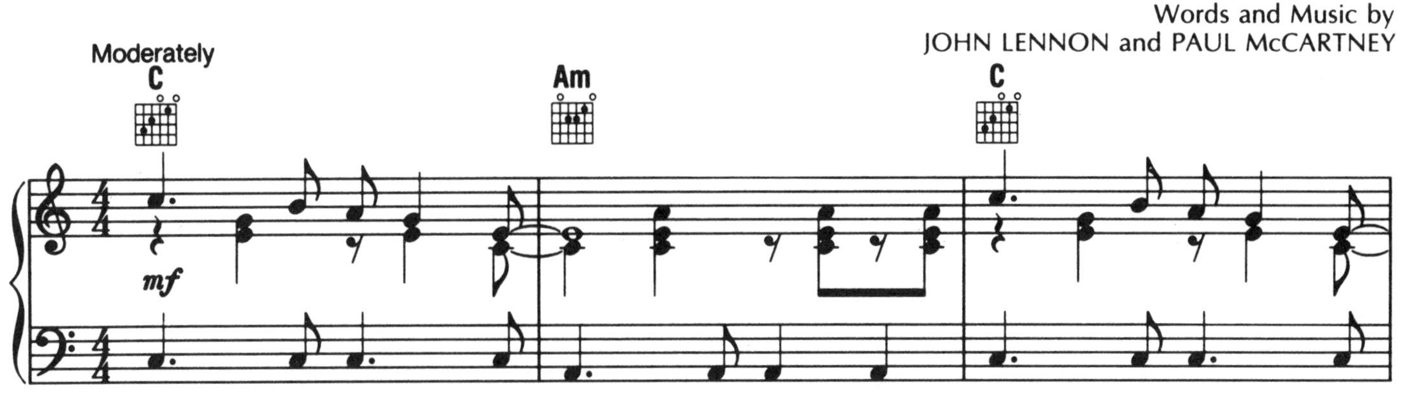

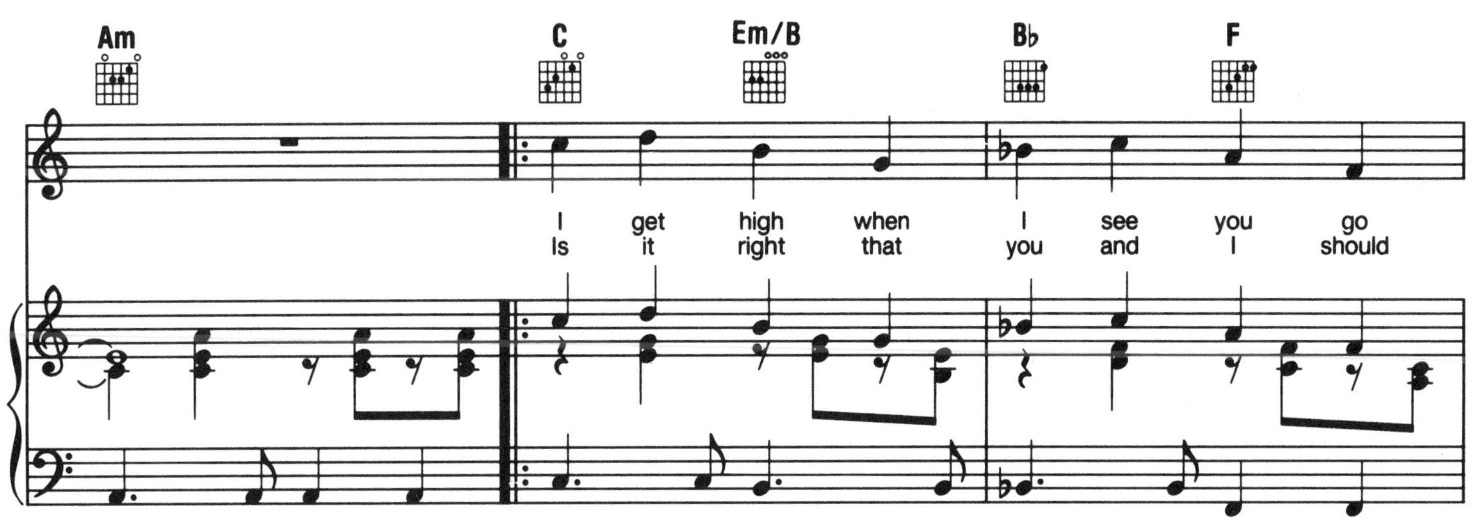

Bb
F
G7sus
G7
G+
my in - side just flies,
you makes night - time bright,
but-ter - flies.
ver - y bright.
F
G
C
Why am I so shy when I'm be - side you?
Hav - en't I the right to make it up girl?
Am
Bb
G7
It's on - ly love and that is all,
Why should I feel
C
Am
Bb
the way I do?
It's on - ly love, and that is all,

G7
F
1 G7
but it's so hard lov - ing you.
2 G7
F
G7
you, Yes, it's so hard lov - ing you lov - ing
C
Am
C
you.
Am
C
Am
C

LADY MADONNA

Words and Music by
JOHN LENNON and PAUL McCARTNEY

F
G
To Coda
A
ends
the
in your
ends
meet.
rest.
head.
meet.
Who
finds
the
mon-
(Instrumental)
(Instrumental)
D
A
D
- ey
when
you
pay
the
rent,
A
F
G
Did
you
think
that
mon - ey
was
heav
-
ven
sent?

A
Dm7
Fri - day night arrives with - out a
3. Tues - day af - ter - noon is nev - er

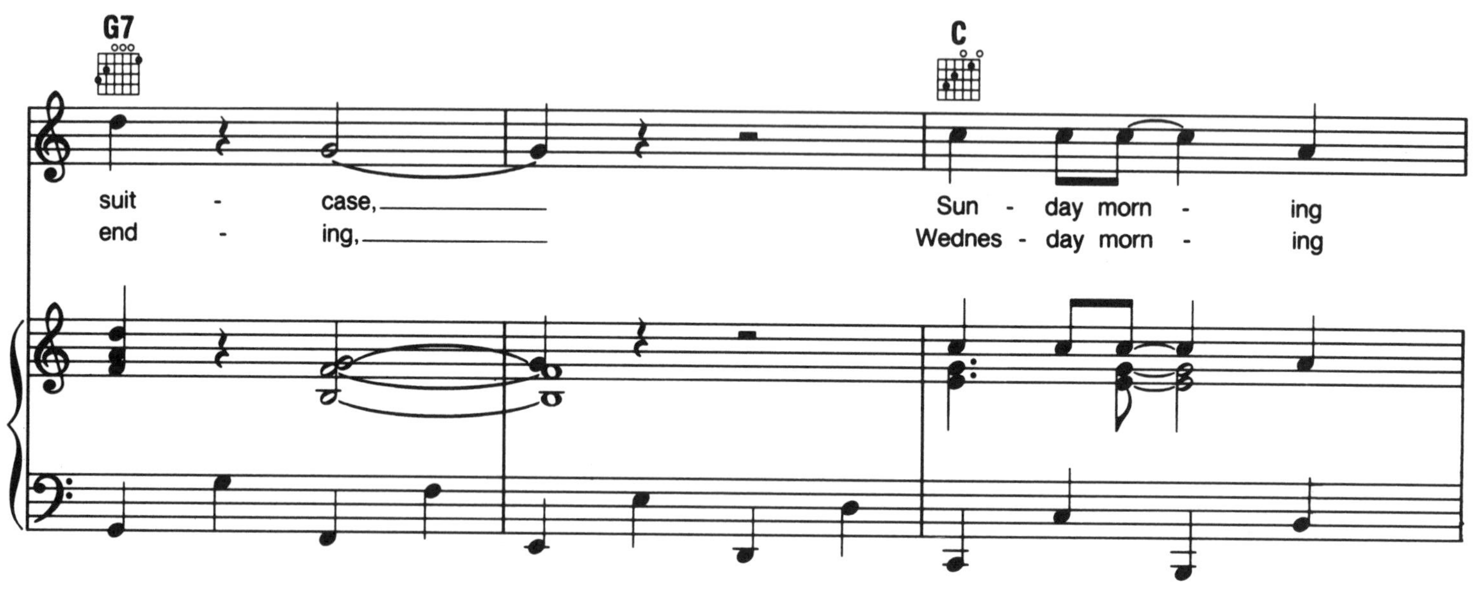
G7
C
suit - case,
end - ing,
Sun - day morn - ing
Wednes - day morn - ing

Am
Dm7
creep - ing like a nun,
pa - pers did - n't come,
Mon - day's child has
Thurs - day night your

G7
learned to tie his boot - lace.
stock - ings need - ed mend - ing.
C
Bm7
D/E
1,2
E7
3
E7
D.S. al Coda
See how they run!
CODA
A
Bm
Cdim
E7sus
A
A
Bm
Cdim
E7sus
A

LET IT BE

Words and Music by
JOHN LENNON and PAUL McCARTNEY

Am G F C G
stand-ing right in front of me Speak-ing words of wis - dom, Let it
F C/E Dm7 C Am G
be. Let it be, let it be, let it be,
Let it be, let it be, let it be,
F C G
let it be, Whis-per words of wis - dom, Let it be.
let it be, Whis-per words of wis - dom, Let it be.
F C/E Dm7 C G
And when the bro - ken - heart - ed peo - ple
And when the night is cloud - y there is

Am G F C G
liv - ing in the world a - gree There will be an an - swer, Let it
still a light that shines on me Shine un - til to - mor - row. Let it
F C/E Dm7 C G
be.
be.
For though they may be part - ed there is
I wake up to the sound of mu - sic
Am G F C G
still a chance that they will see There will be an an - swer, Let it
Moth - er Mar - y comes to me Speak - ing words of wis - dom, Let it
F C/E Dm7 C Am G
be.
be.
Let it be, let it be, let it be,

F
C
G
let it be,
There will be an an - swer, Let it be.
F
C/E
Dm7
C
G
Am
G
Let it be, let it be, let it be,
F
C
G
To Coda
let it be,
Whis - per words of wis - dom, let it be.
There will be an an - swer, let it be.
F
C/E
Dm7
C
F
Em
Dm7
C
B♭
F/A

G
F
C
F
C
G
F
C
D.S. al Coda
CODA
F
C/E
Dm7
C
Am
G
Let it be,
let it be,
let it be,
F
C
G
let it be.
Whis-per words of wis - dom, let it be.
F
C/E
Dm7
C
F
Em
Dm7
C
B♭
F/A
G
F
C

LONG TALL SALLY

Words and Music by ENOTRIS JOHNSON,
RICHARD PENNIMAN and ROBERT BLACKWELL

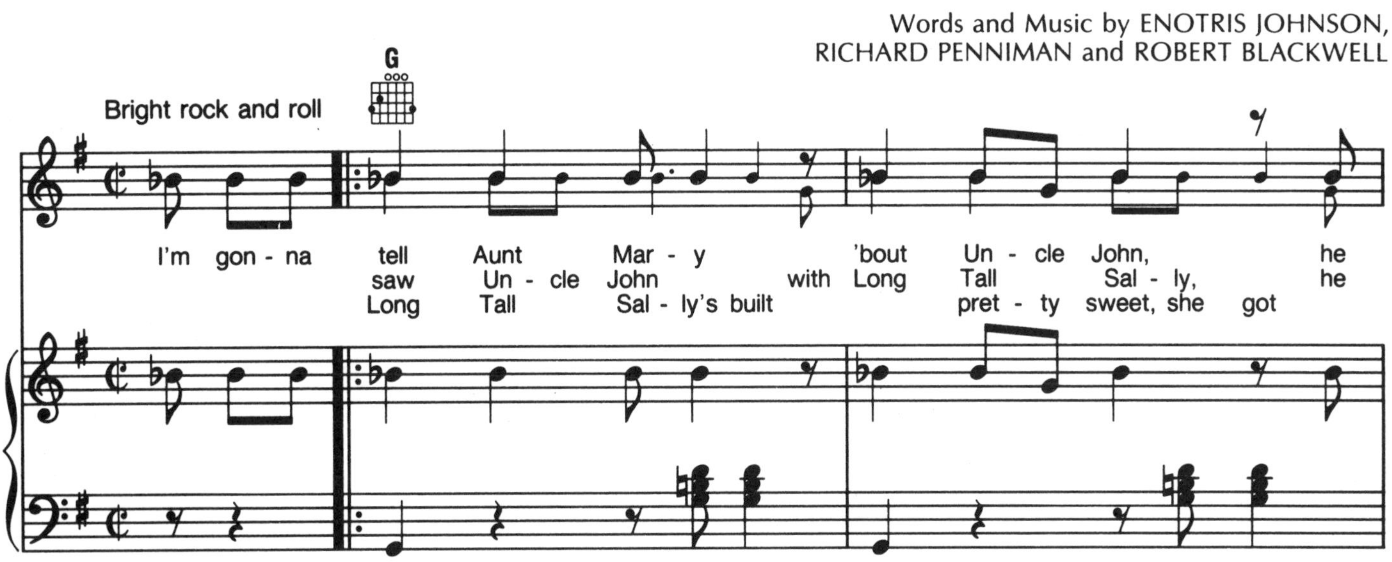

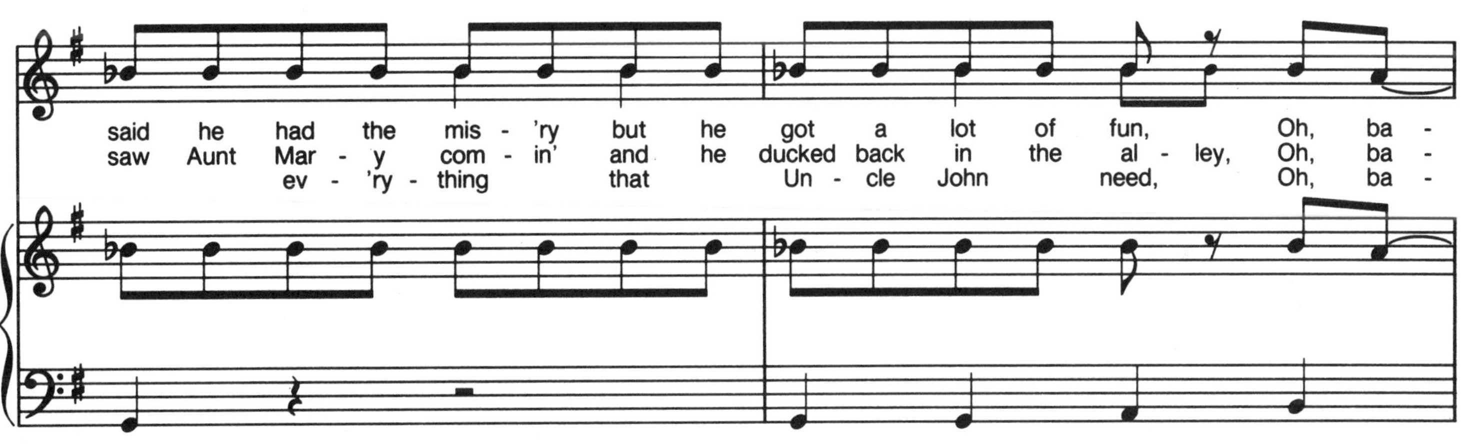

D7
Woo,
ba
-
by,
C7
G
1
D7
some fun to - night.
I
2
D7
G7
C7

G7
D7
C7
G7
D7
3
D7
G7
Well
G♯
A
B♭
B

C
G
D7
C7
G
D7
G
Well we're gon - na have some fun to - night,
have some fun to - night,
(oo)

C7
G
Ev - 'ry - thing's all right,
have some fun to - night,
D7
Have some fun,
(2nd time) Yeah, we'll have some fun,
1
C7
yeah, yeah,
G
D7
yeah,
(Wow)
We're gon - na
2
C7
some fun to - night
G
C
C#dim7
D7
G7
G9

LITTLE CHILD

Words and Music by JOHN LENNON
and PAUL McCARTNEY

F#7
B7
Ba-by take a chance with me.
F#7
B7
Lit-tle child, ba-by take a chance with me.
E
E
If you want some-one to make you
by my side you're the
B
feel so fine, then we'll
on-ly one, don't you
E
have some fun when you're
run and hide, just come
E7
mine all mine. So come
on, come on. Yeah, come
F#
on, come on, come
on, come on, come

B
E7
on,
on,
Lit - tle child,
lit - tle child,
lit - tle child,
E
A
E7
B7
won't you dance with me?
I'm so sad and
A
F#7
B7
To Coda
E7
lone - ly,
ba - by take a chance with me.
Wow! (shout)
E7

A7
E7
B7
A7
F#7
B7
D.S. al Coda
When you're
CODA
E
C#7
F#7
B7
E
C#7
Repeat and Fade
Oh, yeah,
ba - by take a chance with me.
Oh, yeah,

THE LONG AND WINDING ROAD

Words and Music by JOHN LENNON
and PAUL McCARTNEY

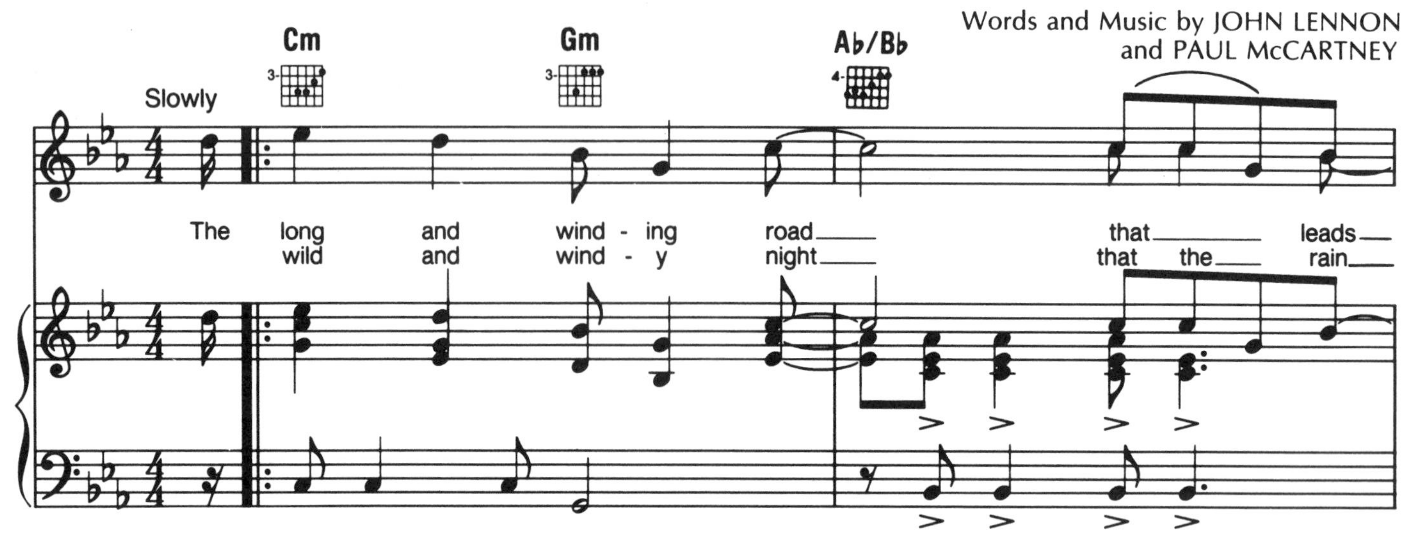

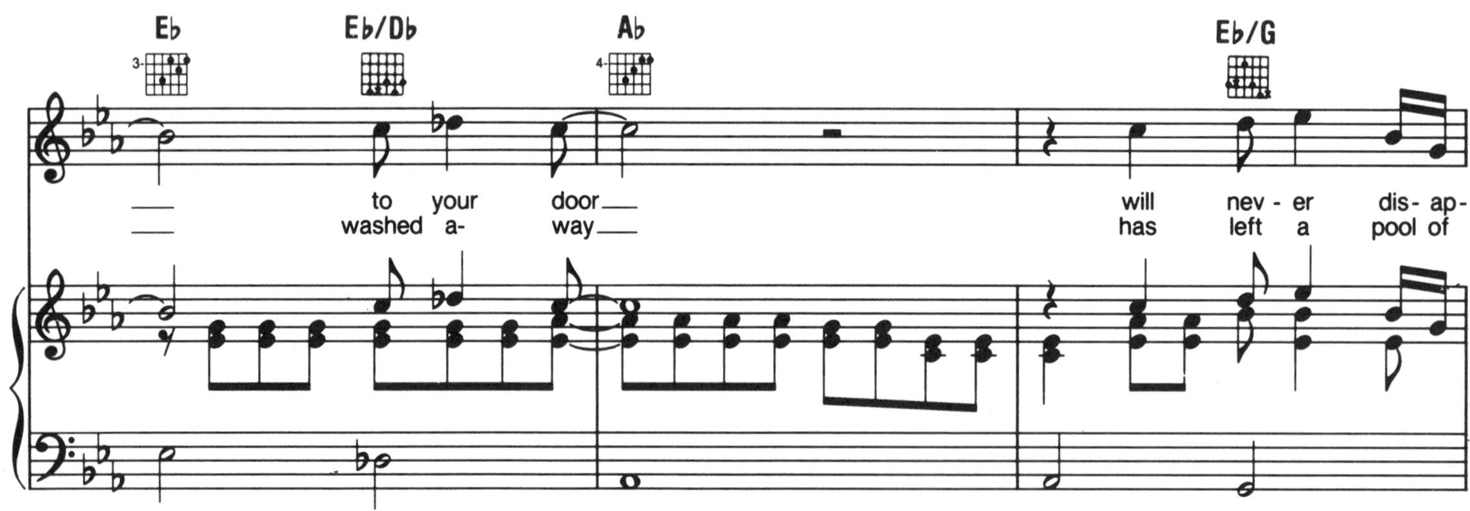

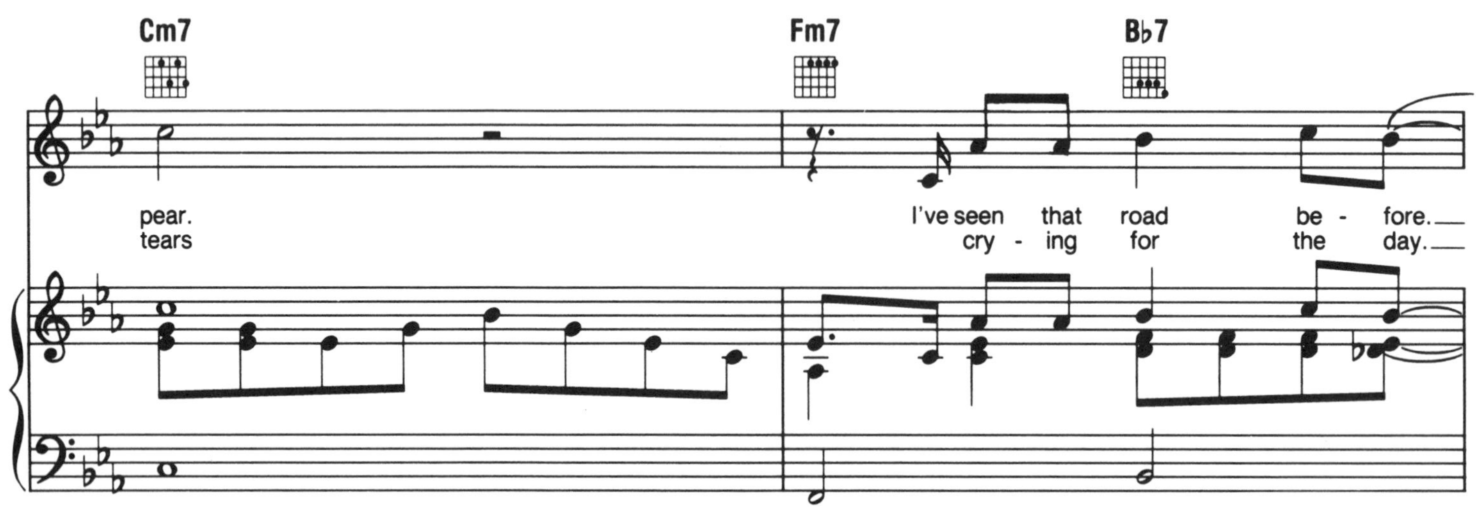

Eb7sus
Eb7
Ab
Eb/G
It always leads
Why leave me standing
Cm
Cm7
Fm7
Bb7
Eb
me here. Lead me to your door. The
here? Let me know the
Eb
Eb/Bb
Ab
way. Many times I've been alone and
Eb/G
Fm7
Bb7
Eb/Bb
Ab
many times I've cried. Anyway you'll never know the

Eb/G
Fm7
Cm
Gm
many ways I've tried. And still they lead me back
Ab/Bb
Eb
Eb/Db
to the long winding road.
Ab
Eb/G
Cm7
You left me standing here
Fm7
Bb7
Eb7sus
Eb7
a long, long time ago.

Ab
Eb/G
Cm
Cm7
Don't
leave
keep
me
wait
-
ing
here.
Fm7
Bb7
To Coda
Eb
Eb/Bb
Ab
Lead me to your door.
Eb/G
Fm7
Eb/Bb
Ab
Eb/G
Fm7
Bb7
D.S. al Coda
But
CODA
Eb
Ab/Bb
Eb
door.
Yeah, yeah, yeah, yeah.

LONG LONG LONG

Words and Music by
GEORGE HARRISON

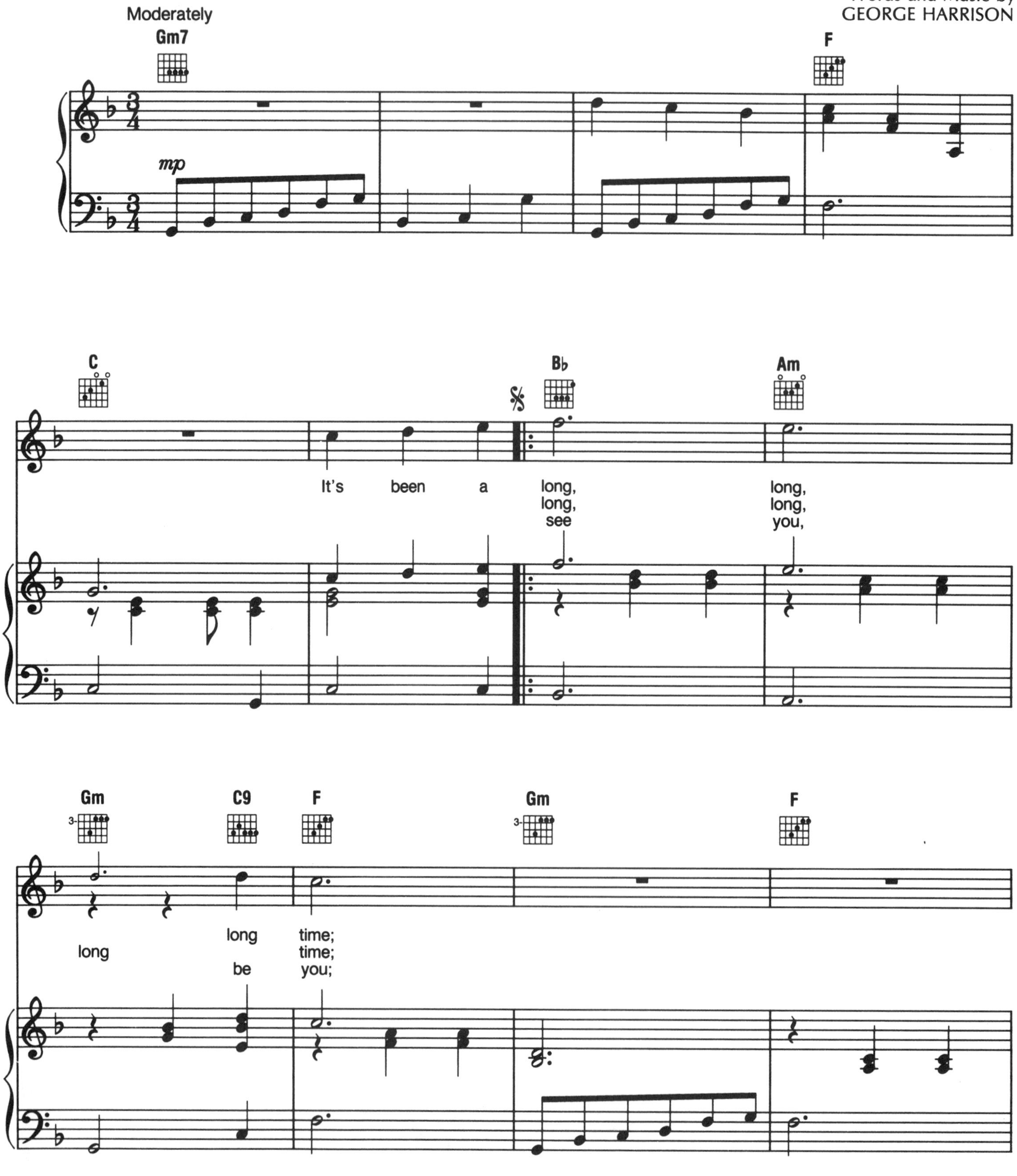

Moderately

Gm7 F

mp

C Bb Am

It's been a long, long,
long, long,
see you,

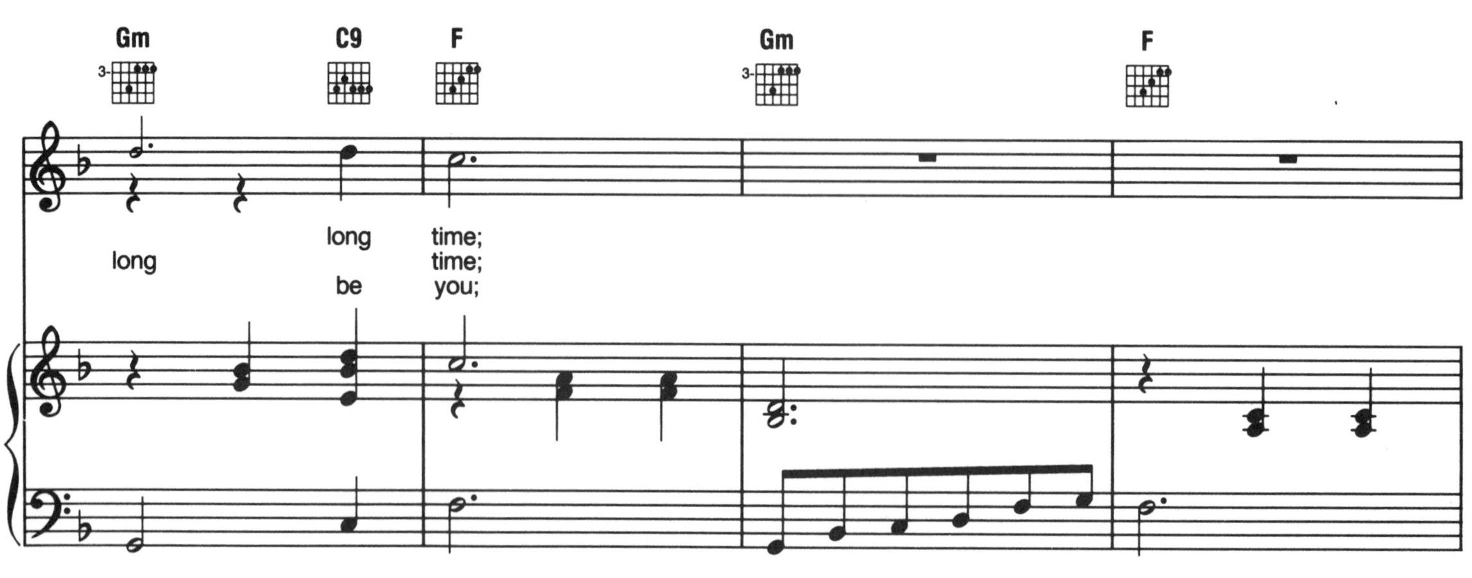

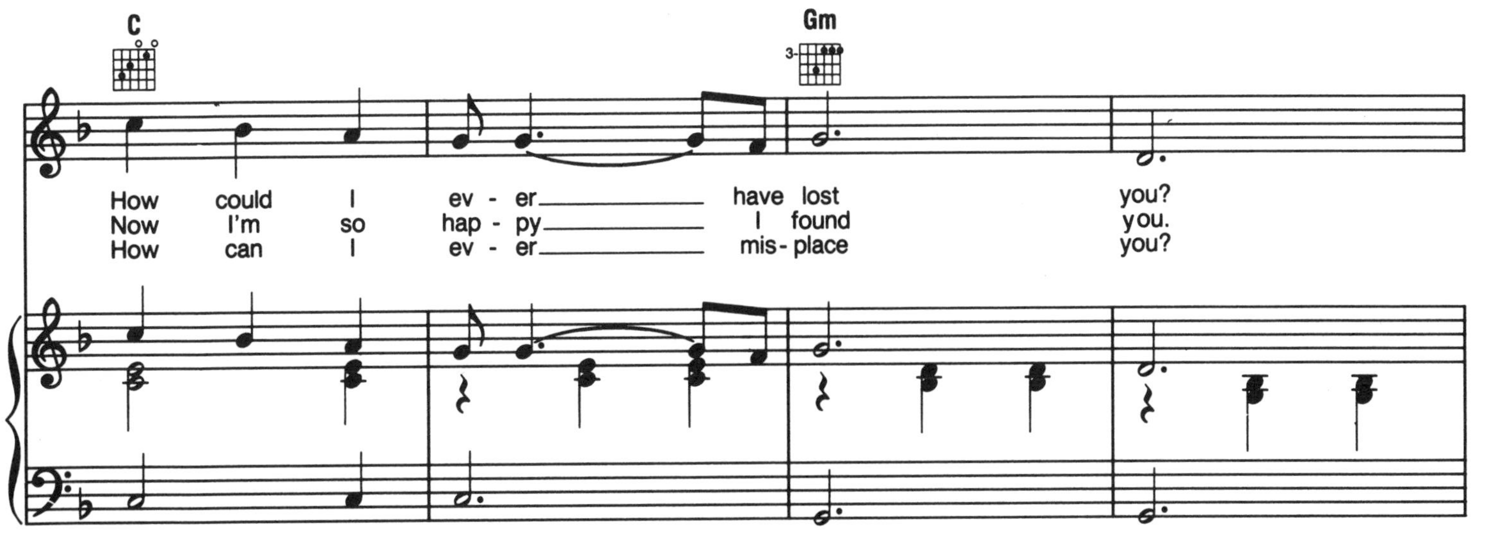
C
Gm
How could I ev - er have lost you?
Now I'm so hap - py I found you.
How can I ev - er mis-place you?

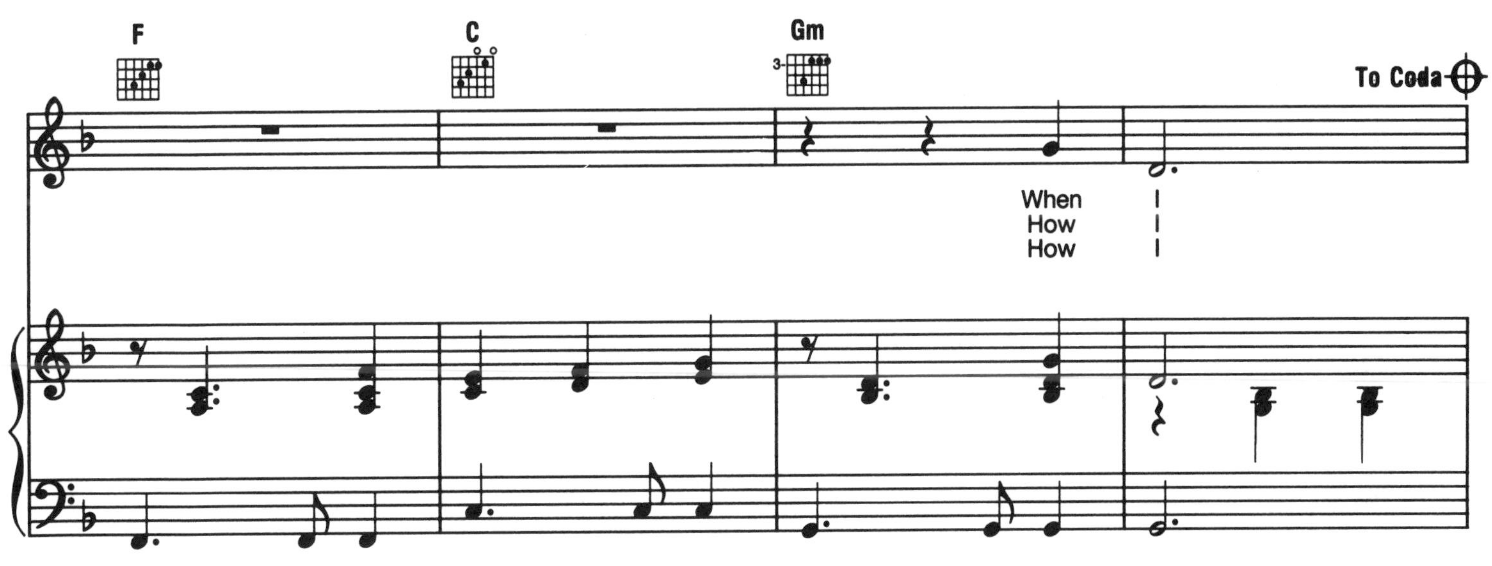
F
C
Gm
To Coda
When I
How I
How I

F
C7
1
loved you.
love you.
It took a

2
B♭
F
C
So man - y years; I was search - ing.
Gm
B♭
So man - y
F
C
Gm
B♭
tears I was wast - ing.
Oh,
C
oh.
D.S. al Coda
Now I can

CODA
F
C
Gm
want
you!
Oh,
I
F
C
Gm
love
you!
You
know
that
I
F
C
Gm
need
you!
Ooh,
I
F
C
love
you.

LOVE ME DO

Words and Music by
JOHN LENNON and PAUL McCARTNEY

no chord
G7
C/D
C
Love me do.
Woh, love
1
2
G
me do.
D
Csus
Some - one to love,
some - bod - y new.
(Instrumental)
no chord
Some - one to love,
some - one like you.

G7
C
G7
Love, love me do, you know I love you,
C
G7
C
I'll al - ways be true, so please
no chord
G7
C/D
1
C
Love me do. Woh, love
G7
C/D
G
me do.
2
C
G7
C/D
Repeat and Fade
Woh, love me do.

LOVELY RITA

Words and Music by
JOHN LENNON and PAUL McCARTNEY

E B C#m F#7 B
noth-ing can come be-tween us; When it gets dark, I tow your heart a - way.
E A D G
Stand-ing by a park-ing me - ter, when I caught a glimpse of Ri - ta,
Took her out and tried to win_ her, had a laugh, and o - ver din - ner
E B E A
fill-ing in a tick-et in her lit-tle white book. In a cap she looked much old - er,
told her I would real-ly like to see her a - gain. Got the bill and Ri - ta paid_ it,
D G E B
and the bag a-cross her shoul - der made her look a lit-tle like a mil-i-t'ry man._
took her home, I near-ly made_ it, sit-ting on the so-fa with a sis-ter or two._

E C#m F#m7 B7 E D A
Love - ly Ri - ta, me - ter maid,
Oh, Love - ly Ri - ta, me - ter maid,
E D C#m F#7
To Coda
may I en - quire dis - creet - ly, "When are you free to take some tea with
where would I be with - out you? Give us a wink and make me think of
B A/B G#m/B F#m/B E6/B B7
me?" Ah. Ri - ta
E D A E B7
6

E
F#7
B7
D.S. al Coda
CODA
B
A
you.
Love - ly Ri - ta, me - ter maid,
E
B
Love - ly Ri - ta, me - ter maid.
A
E
Love - ly Ri - ta, me - ter maid,
Love - ly Ri - ta,

B
Am
me - ter maid.

LOVE YOU TO

Words and Music by
GEORGE HARRISON

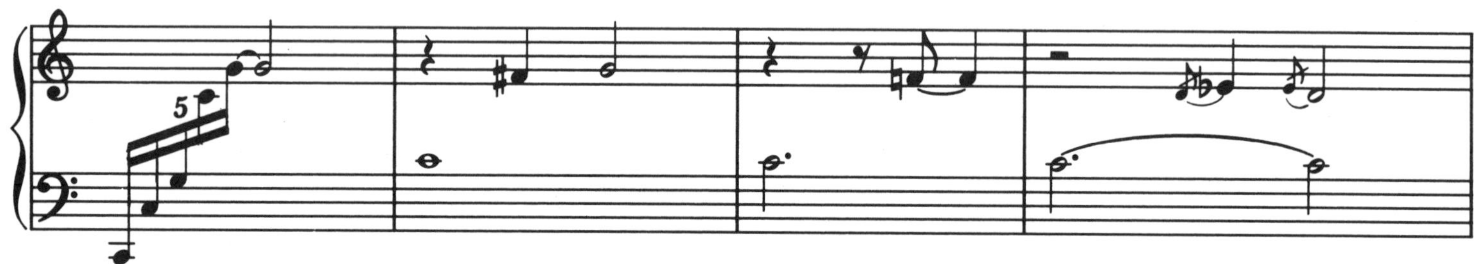

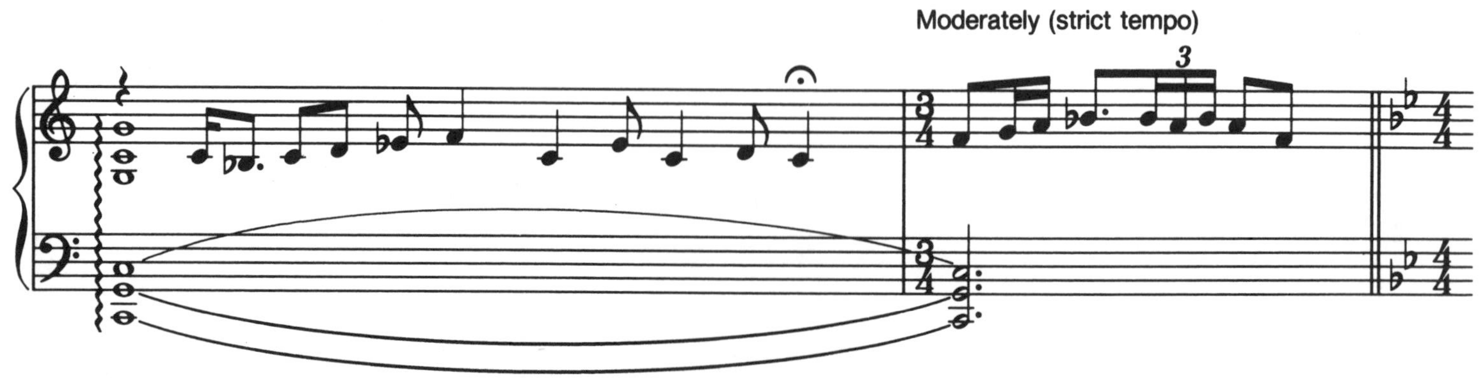

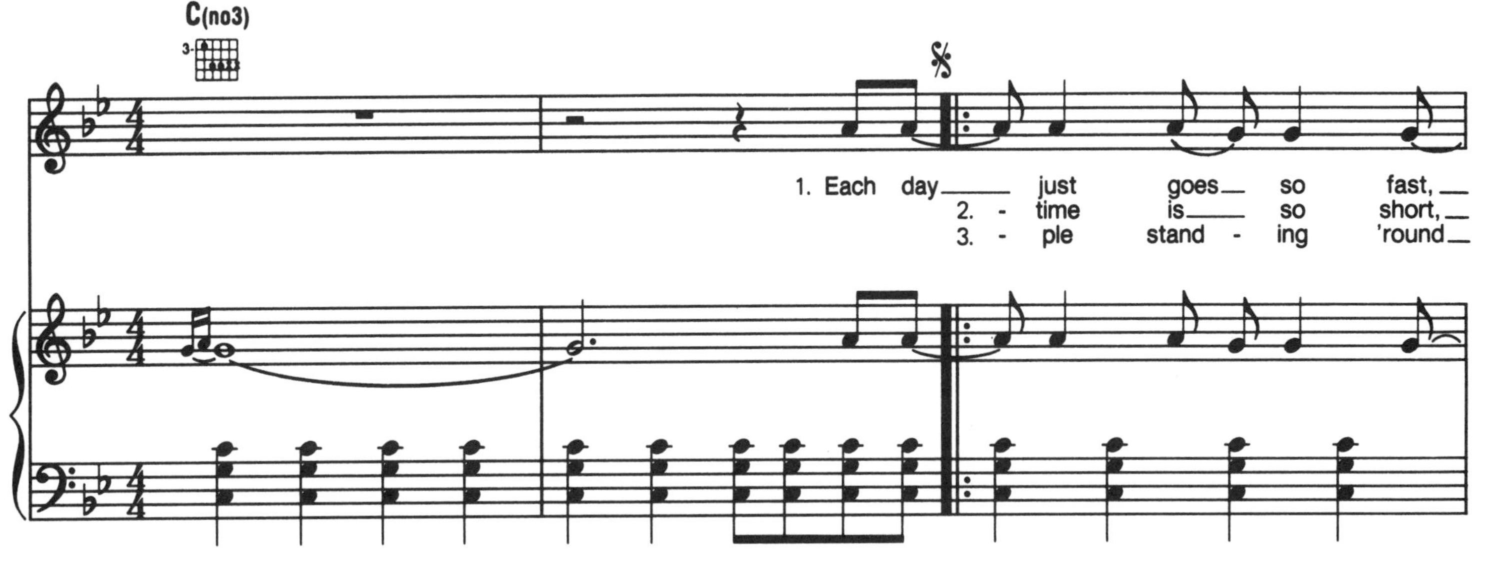
C(no3)
1. Each day just goes so fast,
2. - time is so short,
3. - ple stand - ing 'round

I turn a - round, it's past,
A new one can't be bought.
Who'll screw you in the ground,

You don't get time to hang
But what you've got means such
They'll fill you in with all

a sign on me.
a lot to me.
their sins, you'll see.

3
Love me while you can.
Make love all day long.
I'll make love to you

3
Whole world in a plan.
Make love sing - ing songs.
If you want me to.

To Coda
1
2
A life -

Make love all day long.
Make love sing - ing songs.
3
D.S. al Coda
There's peo -
CODA
Faster

LUCY IN THE SKY WITH DIAMONDS

Words and Music by
JOHN LENNON and PAUL McCARTNEY

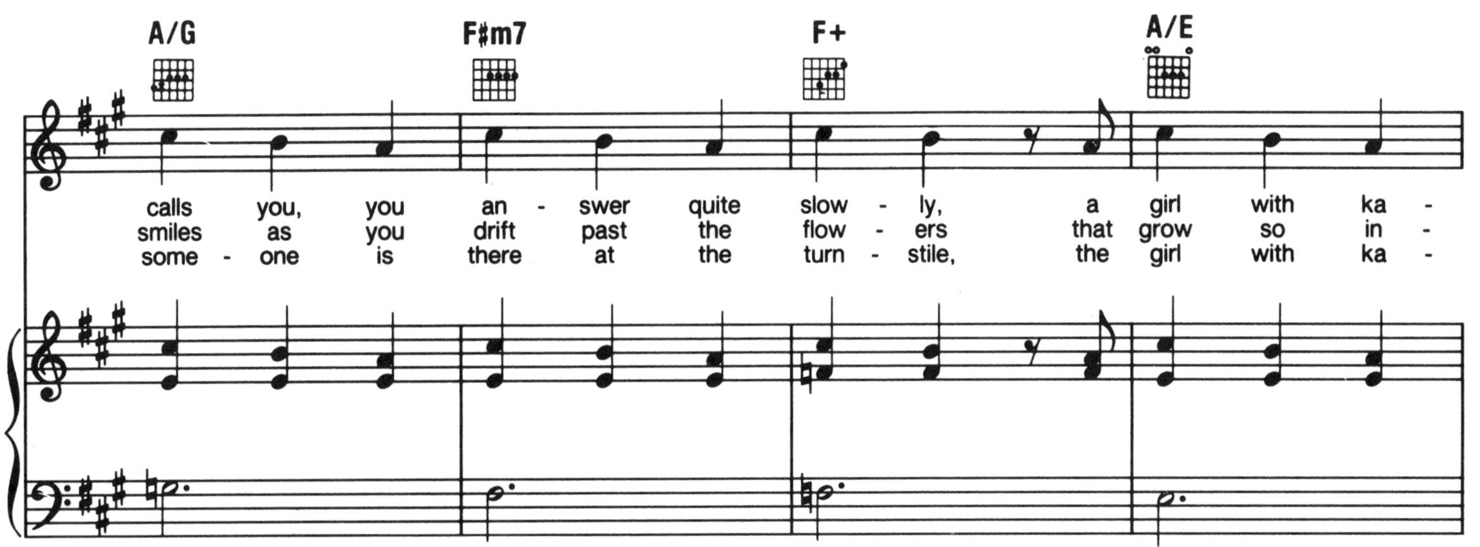
A/G
F♯m7
F+
A/E
calls you, you an - swer quite slow - ly, a girl with ka -
smiles as you drift past the flow - ers that grow so in -
some - one is there at the turn - stile, the girl with ka -

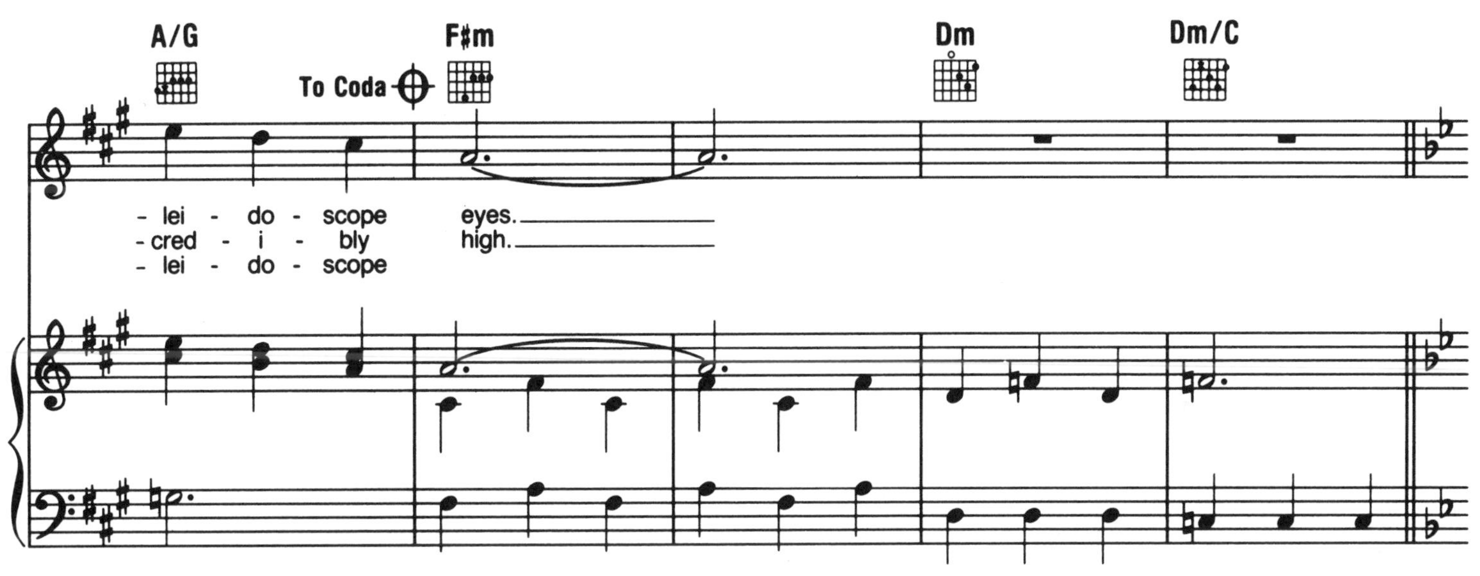
A/G
F♯m
Dm
Dm/C
To Coda
- lei - do - scope eyes.
- cred - i - bly high.
- lei - do - scope

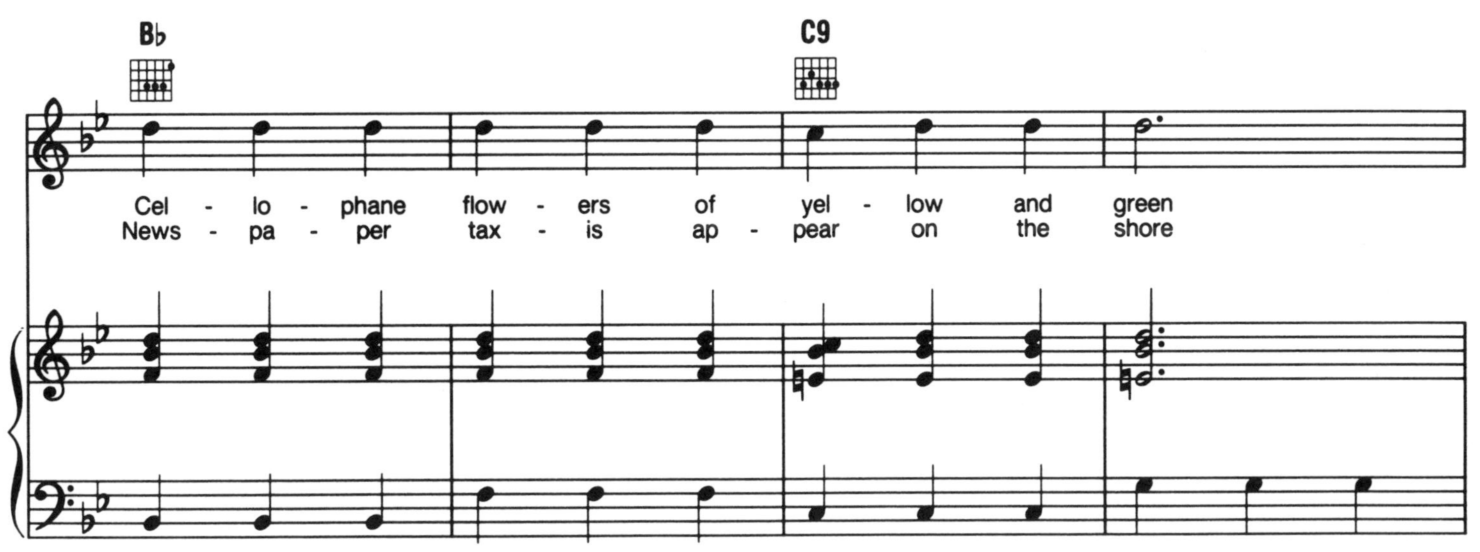
B♭
C9
Cel - lo - phane flow - ers of yel - low and green
News - pa - per tax - is ap - pear on the shore

F6
B♭
C6
tow - er - ing o - ver your head.
wait - ing to take you a - way
Look for the
Climb in the
G
D7
Em
(𝅗𝅥. = 𝅗𝅥)
D
girl with the sun in her eyes and she's gone.
back with your head in the clouds and you're gone.
G
C
D7
G
C
Lu - cy in the sky with dia - monds,
Lu - cy in the sky with
D7
G
C
D7
dia - monds,
Lu - cy in the sky with dia - monds,

1
D
2
D
D.S. al Coda
CODA
F♯m
Ah
Ah
eyes.
G
C
D7
Lu - cy in the sky with dia - monds,
G
C
D7
G
C
Lu - cy in the sky with dia - monds,
Lu - cy in the sky with
D7
D
A
Repeat and Fade
dia - monds,
Ah

MAGGIE MAE

Arrangement by JOHN LENNON, PAUL McCARTNEY,
GEORGE HARRISON and RICHARD STARKEY

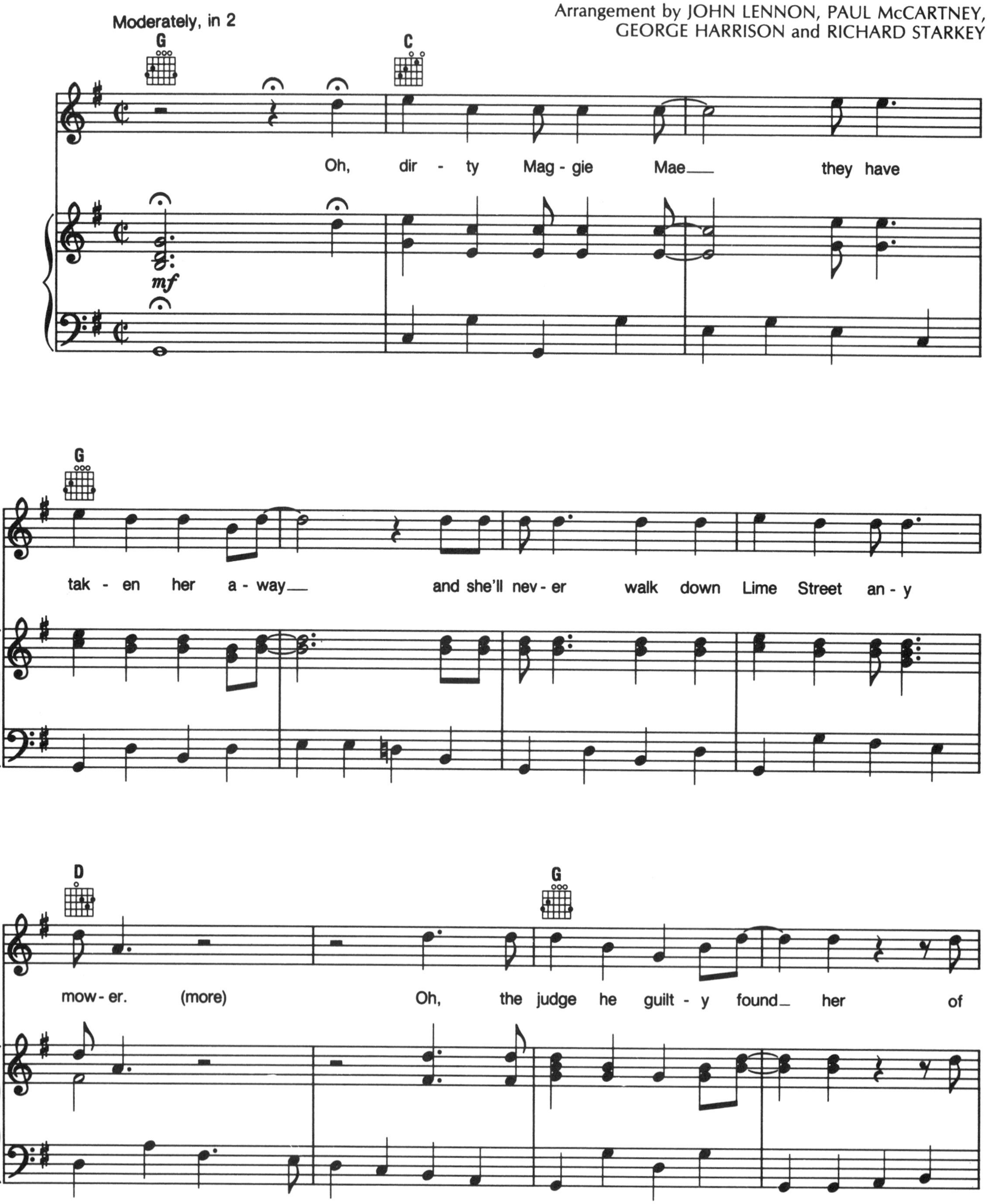
Moderately, in 2
G
C
Oh, dir - ty Mag - gie Mae__ they have
mf
G
tak - en her a - way__ and she'll nev - er walk down Lime Street an - y
D
G
mow - er. (more) Oh, the judge he guilt - y found__ her of

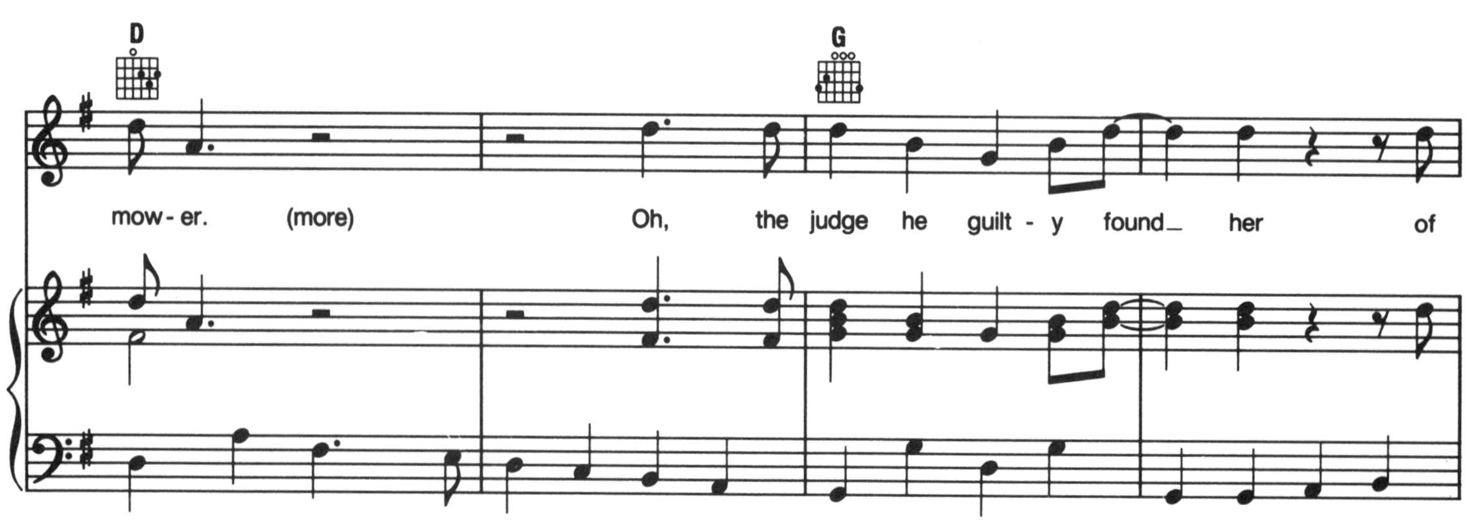

C
D7
rob - bing the home - ward bound - er that dir - ty, no good
G
C
rob - bin' Mag - gie Mae. 'Tis the part of Liv - er - pool
G
she re - turned me to two pound ten a week,
C
G/B
D
that was my pay.

MAGICAL MYSTERY TOUR

Words and Music by
JOHN LENNON and PAUL McCARTNEY

G
A
E
Roll up for the mys - ter - y tour.
(1.3.) Roll up and that's an in - vi - ta - tion,
(2.) Roll up, we've got ev - 'ry - thing you need,
G
A
Roll up for the mys - ter - y tour.
Roll up for the mys - ter - y tour.
E
G
To Coda
Roll up, to make a res - er - va - tion,
Roll up, sat - is - fac - tion guar - an - teed
Roll up for the mys - ter - y tour.
Roll up for the mys - ter - y tour.
A
D
D/C
The Mag - i - cal Mys - ter - y Tour is
The Mag - i - cal Mys - ter - y Tour is

G/B
Gm/B♭
D/A
wait - ing to take you a - way,
hop - ing to take you a - way,
wait - ing to take you a -
Hop - ing to take you a -
A
A
B
way.
way.
F♯m
B
The mys - ter - y trip.
F♯m
A
B
D.S. al Coda
The mys - ter - y trip.

CODA
A
D
D/C
-ter-y tour.
-ter-y tour.
The Mag-i-cal Mys-ter-y
The Mag-i-cal Mys-ter-y
G/B
Gm/B♭
Tour is com-ing to take you a-way.
Tour is dy-ing to take you a-way.
D/A
A6
Com-ing to take you a-way.
Dy-ing to take you a-
A6
D
way, take you to-day.

MARTHA MY DEAR

Words and Music by
JOHN LENNON and PAUL McCARTNEY

Dm
Gm
C7
F
though I spend my days in con - ver - sa - tion, please,
Bb
Ab
re - mem - ber me.
Mar - tha, my love.
Bb7
Ab
Bb7
don't for - get me,
Ab
Bb7
Mar - tha, my dear.

Dm7
Gm9
Hold your head up, you sil - ly girl;
Hold your hand out, you sil - ly girl;
F6
Look what you've done.
See what you've done.
Gm/C
When you find your - self in the
When you find your - self in the
C7
Gm/C
C7
A
thick of it, help your - self to a bit of what is all a - round
thick of it, help your - self to a bit of what is all a - round

Dm7
Gm7
To Coda
you,
sil - ly girl.
you,
sil - ly girl.
Dm7
G9
Take a good look a - round you,
Dm7
G9
Take a good look, you're bound to see
C11
that you and me were

B♭maj7
Dm7
meant to be for each oth - er,
Gm9
sil - ly girl.
E♭
Gm
Gm/F
C7
F

Bb
Abmaj9
Bb7
Abmaj7
Bb7
Abmaj7
Bb7
D.S. al Coda
CODA
Gm7
Eb
Eb
Dm
Gm
Gm/F
Mar - tha, my dear, you have al - ways been my in - spi -

C7
F
B♭
a - tion; Please be good to me.
A♭
B♭7
A♭
Mar - tha, my love don't for - get me,
B♭7
A♭
B♭7
Mar - tha, my dear.
E♭

MAXWELL'S SILVER HAMMER

Words and Music by
JOHN LENNON and PAUL McCARTNEY

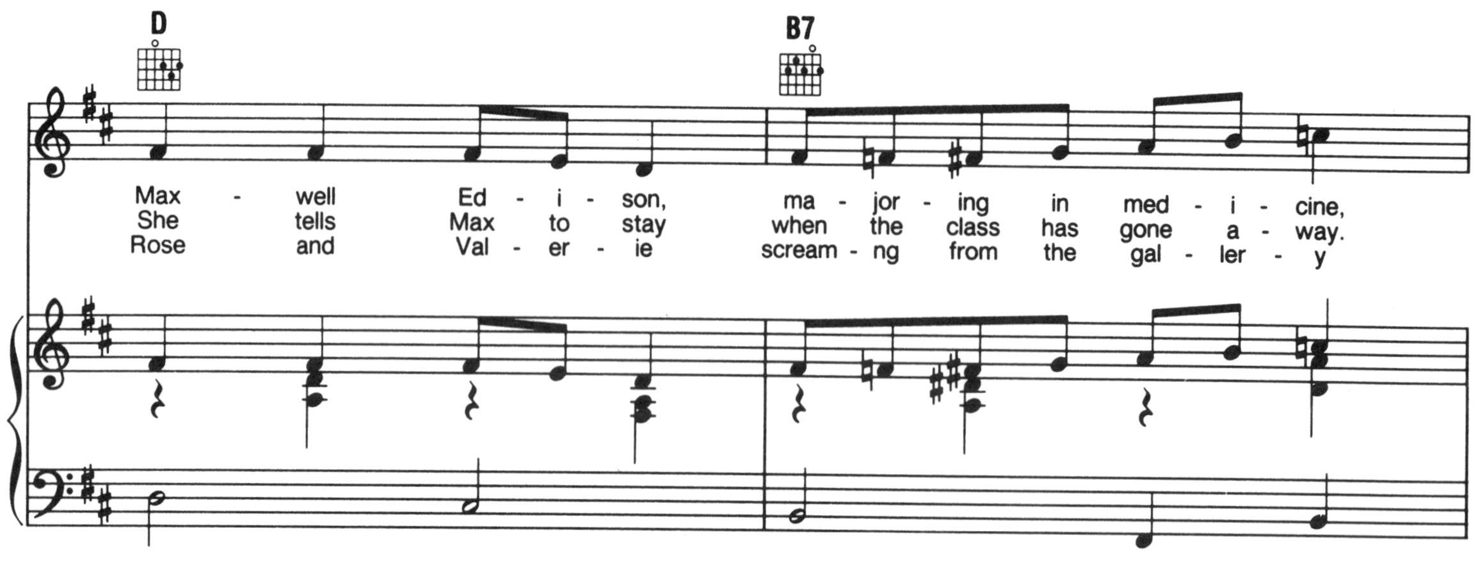
D
B7
Max - well Ed - i - son, ma - jor - ing in med - i - cine,
She tells Max to stay when the class has gone a - way.
Rose and Val - er - ie scream - ng from the gal - ler - y

Em
A7
calls her on the phone:
So he waits be - hind
say he must go free.
"Can I take you out
Writ - ing fif - ty times
The judge does not a - gree

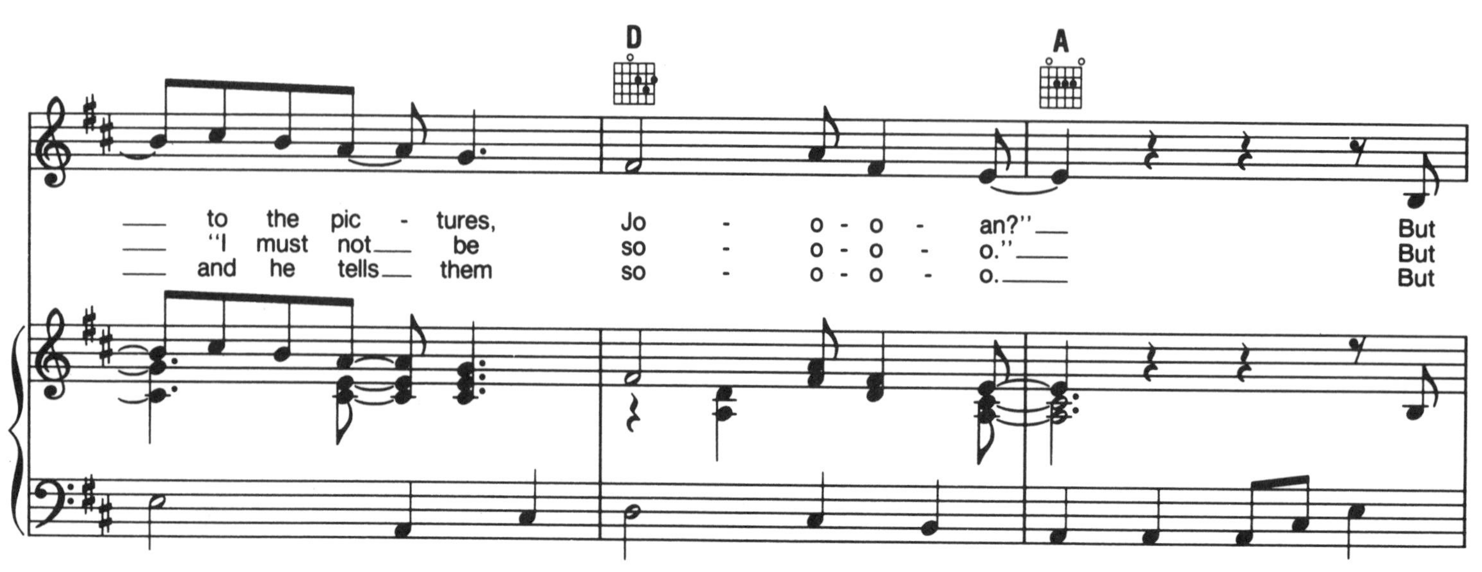
D
A
to the pic - tures, Jo - o - o - an?" But
"I must not be so - o - o - o." But
and he tells them so - o - o - o. But

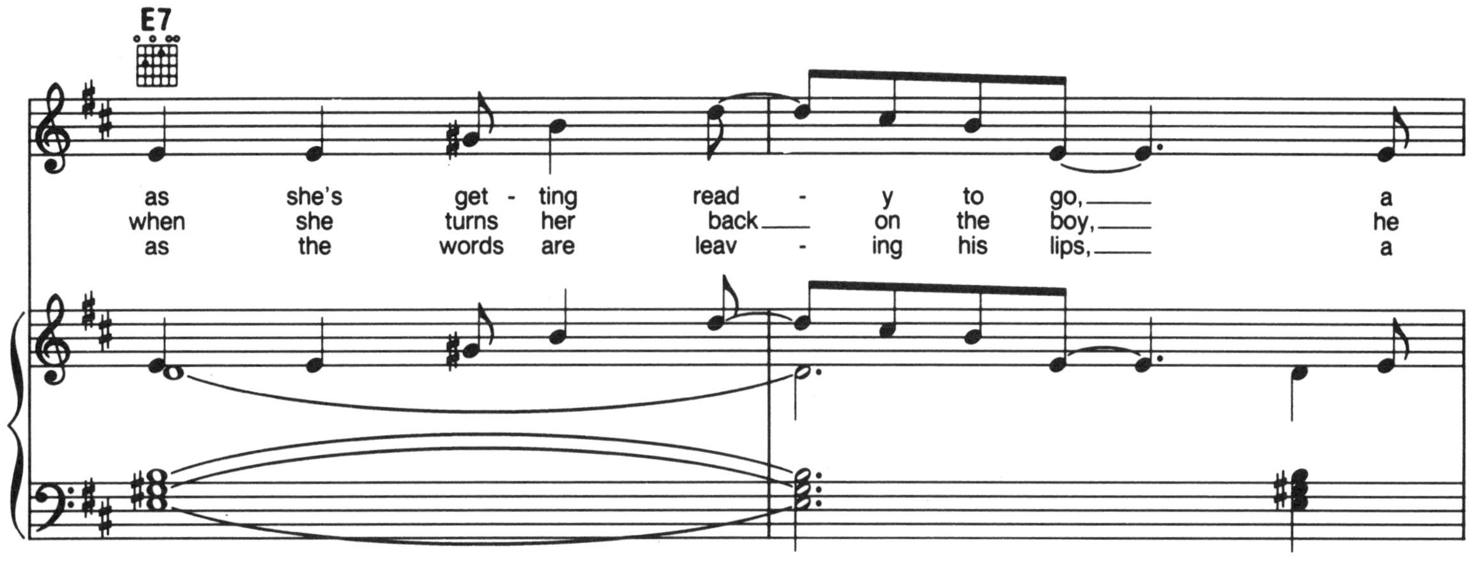
E7
as she's get - ting read - y to go, a
when she turns her back on the boy, he
as the words are leav - ing his lips, a

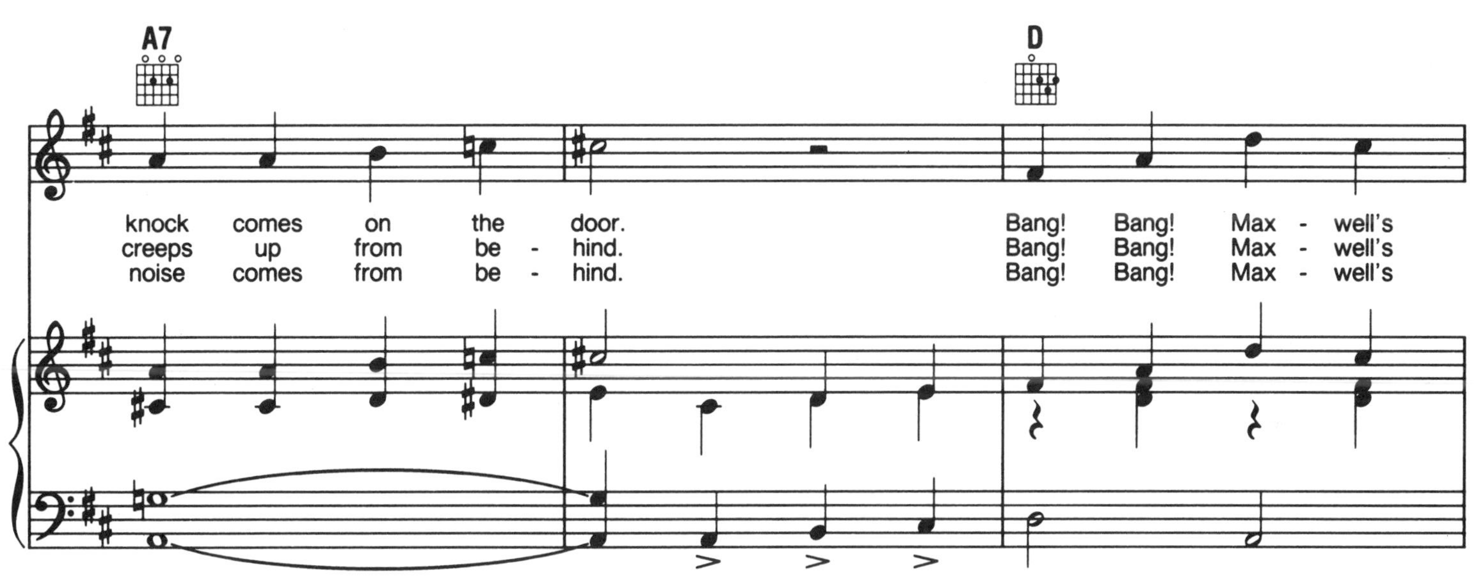
A7
D
knock comes on the door. Bang! Bang! Max - well's
creeps up from be - hind. Bang! Bang! Max - well's
noise comes from be - hind. Bang! Bang! Max - well's

E7
sil - ver ham - mer came down up - on her head.
sil - ver ham - mer came down up - on her head.
sil - ver ham - mer came down up - on his head.

A7
1 Em
A7
Clang! Clang! Max - well's sil - ver ham - mer made sure that she was dead.
Clang! Clang! Max - well's sil - ver ham - mer made
Clang! Clang! Max - well's sil - ver ham - mer made
D
F♯7
Bm
D7
G
G/B
A7/C♯
D
A7/C♯
D
2,3
Em7
A
sure that she was dead.
D
E

A
Em
A
D
To Coda
F#7/C#
Bm
D7/A
D.C. al Coda
CODA
D
F#7/C#
Bm
D7/A
G
A/C#
D
Sil - ver ham - mer.

MATCHBOX

Words and Music by
CARL LEE PERKINS

Bright Shuffle

E7
D7
To Coda
ain't got no match - es, but I sure got a long way to go.
A
E7
A
I'm an ol' poor boy and I'm a
long way from home;
I'm an ol'
D7
poor boy and I'm a long way from home;

A
E7
I'll nev - er be hap - py, 'cause
D7
A
ev - 'ry - thing I ev - er did was wrong.
E7
A
Well, if you don't want my peach - es, hon - ey,
please don't shake my tree;
3
If you
3

D7
don't want an - y of those peach - es, hon - ey, please don't mess a - round my tree.
A
E7
I got news for you, ba - by,
D7
A
E7
leave me here in mis - er - y.
(Spoken:) All right!
A

D7
A
E7
D7
A
E7
Well, let me be
A
your lit - tle dog till your big dog comes;

D7
Let me be your lit-tle dog
A
till your big dog comes,
And when your
E7
D7
A
big dog gets here, watch how your pup-py dog runs.
E7
D.S. al Coda
Well, I said I'm
CODA
A
A6

MEAN MR. MUSTARD

Words and Music by
JOHN LENNON and PAUL McCARTNEY

D♭7
C7
B7
Keeps a ten bob note up his nose,
Al - ways shouts out some - thing ob - scene,
1
E
C
B7
Such a mean old man,
such a
Such a
E
C
B7
mean old man.
2
E
C
dir - ty old man,
B7
E
C
B7
C7
C♯7
dir - ty old man.

POLYTHENE PAM

Words and Music by
JOHN LENNON and PAUL McCARTNEY

C
D
E
D/E
A
E
Yeah, yeah, yeah.
D/E
A
E
D
A
Get a dose of her in jack-boots and kilt,
E
D
A
E
She's kill-er dill-er when she's dressed to the hilt.
She's the
G
B
C
D
kind of a girl that makes the "News of the World," Yes, you could say she was at-tract-ive-ly built

E
C
D
E
Yeah,
yeah,
yeah.
D/E
A
E
D/E
A
E
D
A
E
D
A
E
D
A
E

D
A
E
D
A
E
D
A
E
D
A
E
D
A
E
D
A
E

SHE CAME IN THROUGH THE BATHROOM WINDOW

Words and Music by
JOHN LENNON and PAUL McCARTNEY

D7
A
banks of her own la - goon.
steal but she could not rob.
Did-n't an - y - bod - y tell
Dm
A
her?
Did-n't an - y - bod - y see?
Dm
G7
C
To Coda
Sun-day's on the phone to Mon - day,
G7
C
A
Tues - day's on the phone to me.
She said she'd al - ways been a

D
A
F#m
danc - er,
she worked in fif - teen clubs a
D
A
F#m
day.
And though she thought I knew the
D
D7
D.S. al Coda
an - swer,
Well, I knew but I could not say.
CODA
G7
C
A
Tues - day's on the phone to me,
oh yeah!

MISERY

Words and Music by JOHN LENNON
and PAUL McCARTNEY

Am
C
F
C
I've lost her now for sure; I won't see her no
F
G
C
more. It's gon - na be a drag, mis - er - y.
Am
C
I'll re - mem - ber all the lit - tle things we've done.
Am
1. Can't she see she'll al - ways be the
2. She'll re - mem - ber and she'll miss her

G
G7
C
on - ly one,
on - ly one.
on - ly one,
lone - ly one.
Send her back to
F
C
F
me 'cause ev - 'ry - one can see With -
G
1 C
out her I will be in mis - er - y.
2 C
Am
C
Am
Repeat and Fade
mis - er - y. Oh, in mis - er - y. Ooh, my

MICHELLE

Words and Music by
JOHN LENNON and PAUL McCARTNEY

Fm
Ab7sus
love you, I love you, I love you, that's all I want to
need to, I need to, I need to, I need to make you
Db
C7sus
Fm
say. Un - til I find a way, I will
see. Oh, what you mean to me un -
C+
Fm7
Fm6
Dbmaj7/F
1 C
say the on - ly words I know that you'll un - der - stand.
til I do, I'm hop - ing you will know what I
2 C
F
Bbm7
Eb
mean. I love you.

Ddim
C
Bdim
C
Fm
I want you, I want you, I
Ab7sus
Db
C7sus
want you, I think you know by now, I'll get to you some-
Fm
C+
Fm7
Fm6
Dbmaj7/F
how. Un - til I do, I'm tell - ing you, so you'll un - der -
C
F
Bbm7
Eb
stand: Mi - chelle, ma belle, sont des mots qui

Ddim
C
Bdim
C
vont tres bien en - semble, tres bien en - semble. And I will
Fm
C+
Fm7
Fm6
D♭maj7/F
say the on - ly words I know that you'll un - der -
C
F
B♭m7
E♭
stand, my Mi - chelle.
Ddim
C
Bdim
C
F
Repeat and Fade

MONEY (THAT'S WHAT I WANT)

Words and Music by BERRY GORDY, JR.
and JANIE BRADFORD

Em
but you can keep 'em for the birds and bees; Now give me
but your lov - in' don't pay my bills; Now give me
what it don't get I can't use; Now give me
A
(Backing):
That's what I want.
Em
That's
A
mon - ey, that's what I want,
Em
what I want.
B7
That's
A7
what I want.
that's what I want yeah,

Em
A
1,2
To Coda
Em
B7
3
Em
B7
That's what I want.
that's what I want.
D.C. al Coda
CODA
Em
B7
Em
A
That's
1, 2. Well, now give me mon - ey,
Em
A
Em
A
Em
A
what I want.
That's
what I want.
A lot - ta mon - ey,
(1.) Oh. yeah. I wan -
(2.) Wo. yeah. You need

Em
A
Em
A
That's
what I
want.
na be
free.
Oh,
mon - ey.
(Oh now) Gim - me
Em
A
Em
B7
That's
what I
want.
That's
lot - ta mon - ey.
mon - ey.
That's what I want
A7
Em
A
Em
what I
want.
yeah,
that's what I want.
3

MOTHER NATURE'S SON

Words and Music by JOHN LENNON
and PAUL McCARTNEY

D
Dm
G/D
D
To Coda
Dm
G/D
D
D
G/D
D
Sit be - side a moun - tain stream,
Find me in my field of grass,
Bm
Bm/A
E9
A
D/A
A
D/A
see her wa - ters rise;
Moth - er Na - ture's son.
Lis - ten to the
Sway - ing dais - es
A
D/A
A
D/A
D
Dm
pret - ty sound of mu - sic as she flies.
sing a la - zy song be - neath the sun.

G/D
D
Du du du du du du du du du du du
du du du du du du du du du,
Dmaj7
D7
Dsus
Gm/D
du du du.
1
D.S. al Coda
CODA
Dm
G
(Hum)
Moth- er Na - ture's son.

THE NIGHT BEFORE

Words and Music by
JOHN LENNON and PAUL McCARTNEY

D
C
G
Love was in your eyes.
Was I so un - wise?
A7
Bm
Gm6
1. Now to - day I find
2,3 When I held you near
Bm
Gm6
D
you have changed your mind,
you were so sin - cere,
Treat me like you did
G7
D
1
F
G
the night be - fore.

2,3
D
Am7
D7
Last night is the night I will re - mem -
G
Bm7
- ber you by;
When I think of things
E7
A7
we did it makes me want to cry.
D
C
G
We said our good - byes
Were you tell - ing lies?

A7
D
C
Love was in your eyes.
Was I so un - wise?
G
A7
Bm
Now to - day I
When I held you
Gm6/Bb
Bm
Gm6
find you have changed your mind,
near you were so sin - cere,
D
G7
To Coda
D
Treat me like you did the night be - fore.

F
G
D
C
G
A7
D
C
G
A7
D
D.S. al Coda
CODA
D
G7
D
Like the night be - fore.
3

MR. MOONLIGHT

Words and Music by
ROY LEE JOHNSON

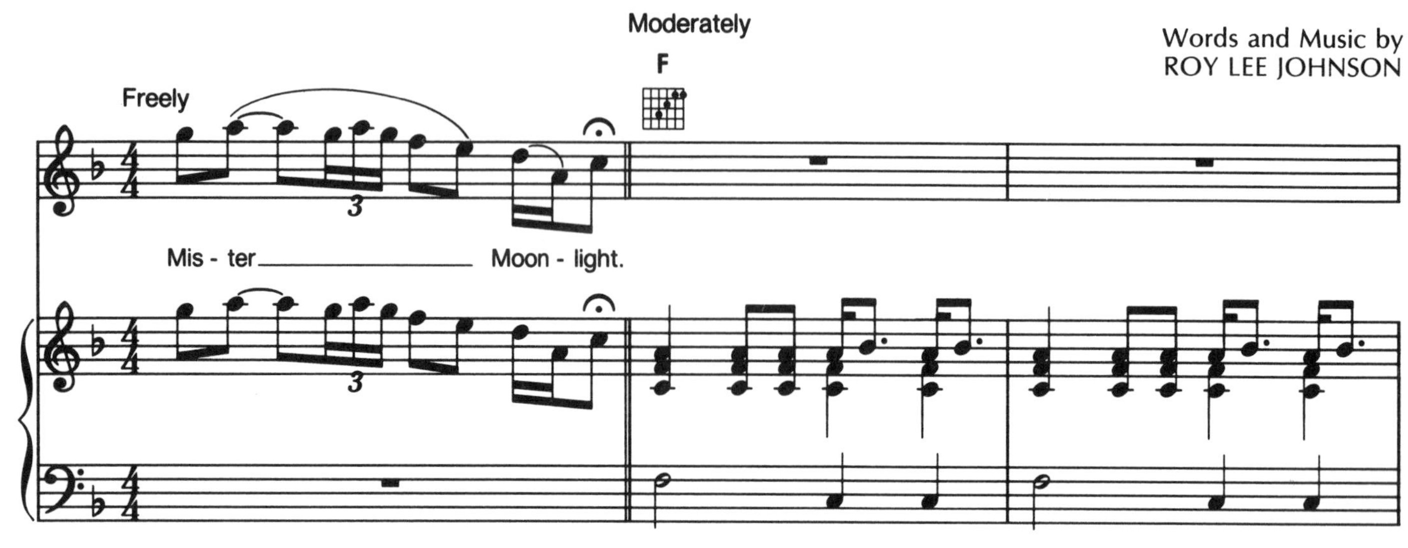

F
Dm
3
dream
And from the
whirl you sent my girl,
B♭
F
And from a - bove you sent us love.
B♭
And now she is mine,

F
D7
Gm7
I think you're fine 'cause we love you
C7
F
Mis - ter Moon - light.
F
Mis - ter Moon - light, come a - gain please,
Here I am on my knees, beg - ging if you

B♭
please.
On the night you don't come
F
my way
I
pray and pray more each
D7
Gm7
C7
To Coda
day, 'cause we love you,
Mis - ter Moon -
F
F
light.

B♭
On the night you don't come
F
my way,
Oh,
I pray and pray more each

D7
Gm7
C7
day, 'cause we love you, Mis - ter Moon -
F
D.S. al Coda
light.
CODA
F
light,
Mis - ter Moon - light, Mis - ter Moon -
light, Mis - ter Moon - light.

NO REPLY

Words and Music by
JOHN LENNON and PAUL McCARTNEY

Am
Em
Fmaj7
Em
I saw the light,
I near - ly died,
Dm7
I know that you saw me, 'cause I looked up to
'Cause you walked hand in hand with an - oth - er
G7
C
To Coda
see your face.
man in my place.
I tried to tel - e -
C
E7
If I were you I'd re - al - ize that
give the lies that

A7 Dm

I love you more than
I heard be - fore when you

F C

an - y oth - er guy.
gave me no re - ply.

1

And I'll for -

2

D.S. al Coda

3. I tried to tel - e -

CODA

C Am Em

No re - ply,

Fmaj7 C6/9

No re - ply.

OCTOPUS'S GARDEN

B
B7
E
shade.
He'd let us in
Rest - ing our head
C♯m
knows where we've been
on the sea - bed
in his
in an
A
B
oct - o - pus - 's gar - den in the shade.
oct - o - pus - 's gar - den near a cave.
C♯m
I'd ask my friends to come and see
We would sing and dance a - round

A
B
an oct - o - pus - 's gar - den with me.
be - cause we know we can't be found.
E
C#m
I'd like to be
un - der the sea
A
B
in an oct - o - pus - 's gar - den in the shade.
1
E
2
E

A
F#m7
D
E
A
F#m7
D
E
A
B

E
C#m
We would shout
and swim a - bout
the cor - al
that lies
be - neath
the waves.
A
B
E
Oh, what joy
C#m
for ev - 'ry girl and boy

A
B
knowing they're happy and they're safe.
C♯m
We would be so
happy you and me;
A
no one there to
B
tell us what to do.

E
C#m
I'd like to be
un - der the sea
in an
A
B
1
C#m
oct - o - pus - 's gar - den with you.
2
C#m
In an
In an
A
B
E
D#
E
oct - o - pus - 's gar - den with you.

NORWEGIAN WOOD
(THIS BIRD HAS FLOWN)

Em
F♯m7
B7
I looked a-round and I no-ticed there was-n't a chair,
told her I did-n't and crawled off to sleep in the bath.
E
Bm7
A
E
I sat on a rug, bid-ing my time, drink-ing her wine.
And when I a-woke I was a-lone, this bird had flown.
Bm7
A
E
We talked un-til two and then she said, "It's time for bed."
So I lit a fire, Is-n't it good Nor-we-gian wood.
Bm7
A
E
rit.

NOT A SECOND TIME

Words and Music by JOHN LENNON
and PAUL McCARTNEY

G
Em
And now you've changed your mind
G
Em
I see no rea - son to change mine; my
D
Am7
D
cryin' is through, oh.
Am7
Bm
You're giv - ing me the same old line,

G
Em
Am7
I'm won - d'ring why.
You hurt me then,
Bm
you're back a - gain;
No,
no,
D7
Em
To Coda
no,
not a sec - ond time!
Am7
Bm
G
Melody in left hand

Em
Am7
Bm
D7
Em
D.C. al Coda
CODA
Em
G
Not a sec - ond time,
Em
G
Em
Repeat and Fade
Not a sec - ond time,
Not a sec - ond

NOWHERE MAN

Words and Music by
JOHN LENNON and PAUL McCARTNEY

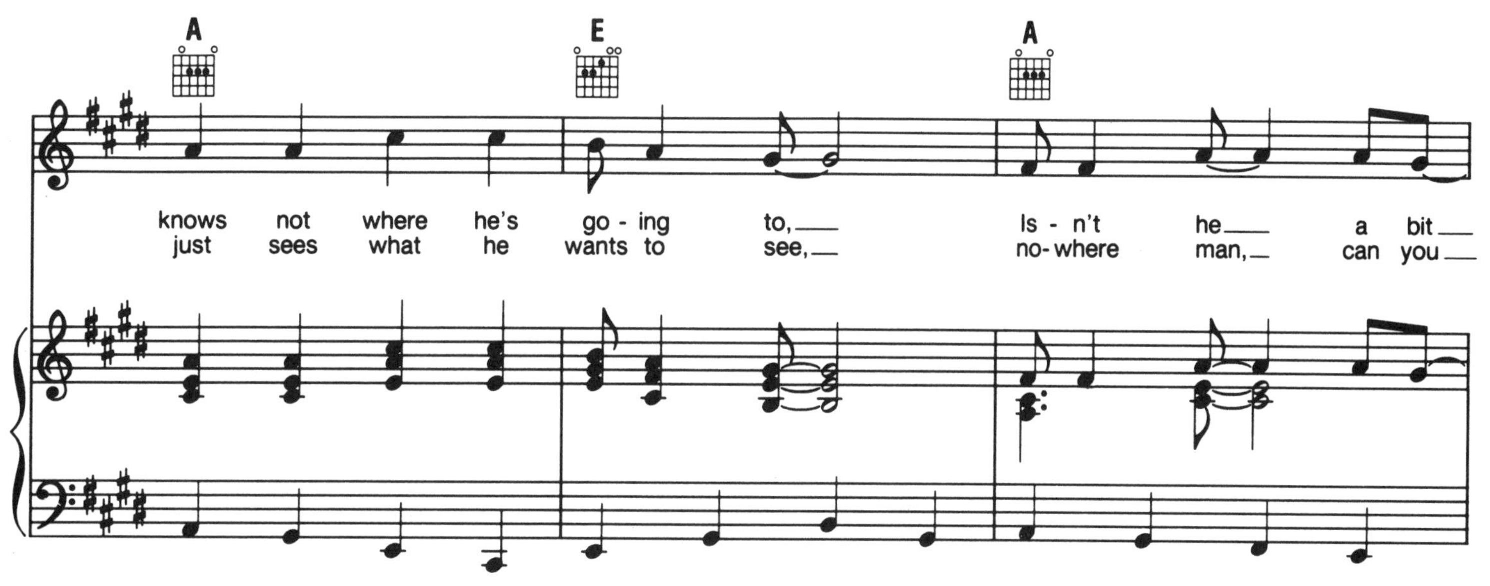
A
E
A
knows not where he's go - ing to,
just sees what he wants to see,
Is - n't he a bit
no-where man, can you

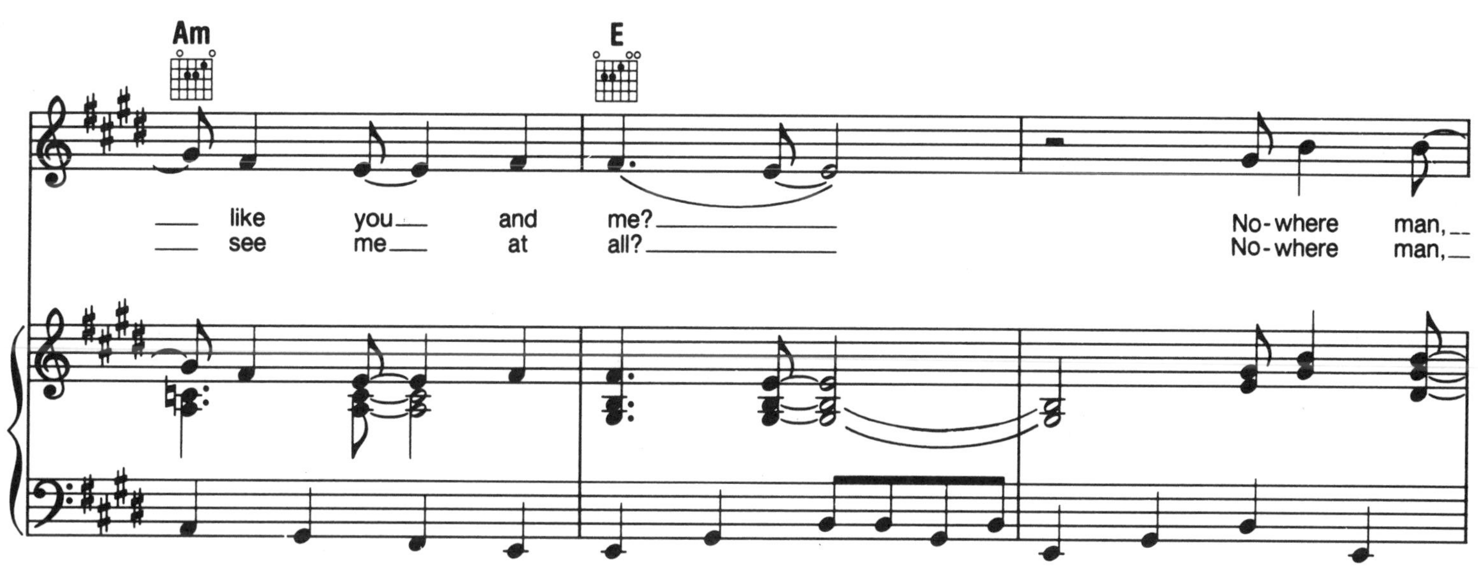
Am
E
like you and me?
see me at all?
No-where man,
No-where man,

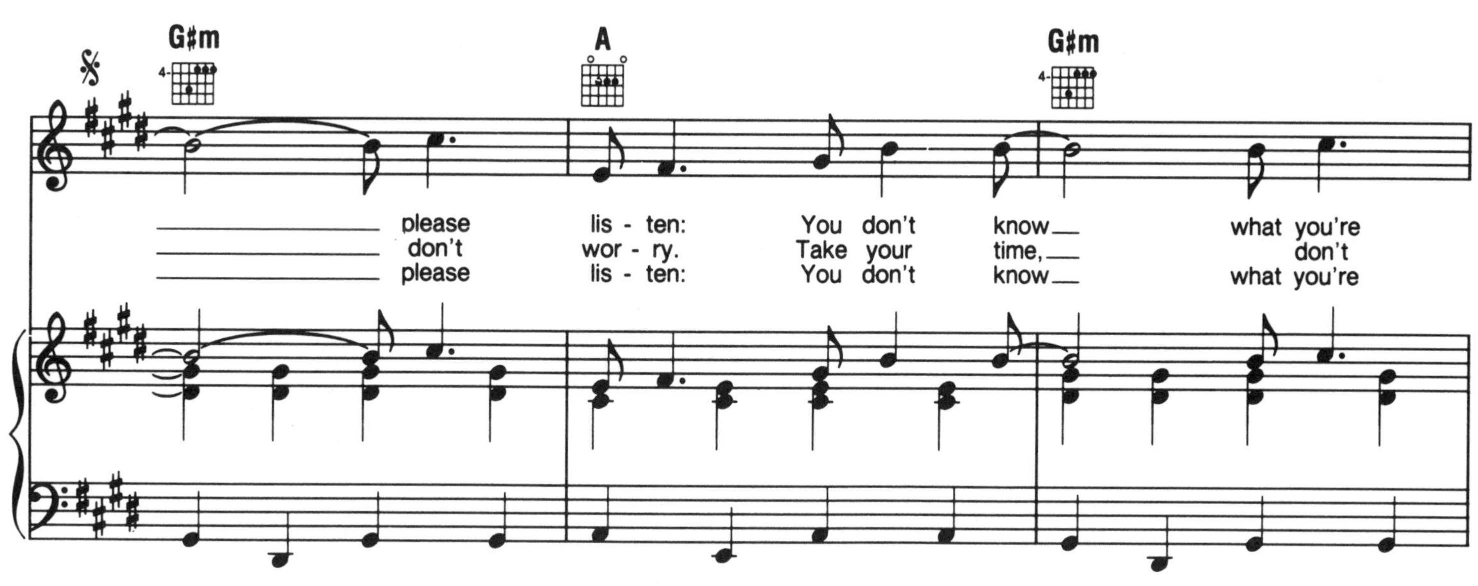
G♯m
A
G♯m
please lis - ten: You don't know what you're
don't wor - ry. Take your time, don't
please lis - ten: You don't know what you're

A
G♯m
F♯m
miss - ing. No- where man, the world is
hur - ry. Leave it all till some - bod - y else
miss - ing. No- where man, the world is

B
E
at your com- mand.
lends you a hand.
at your com- mand.
(Instrumental)
Does - n't have a
He's a real

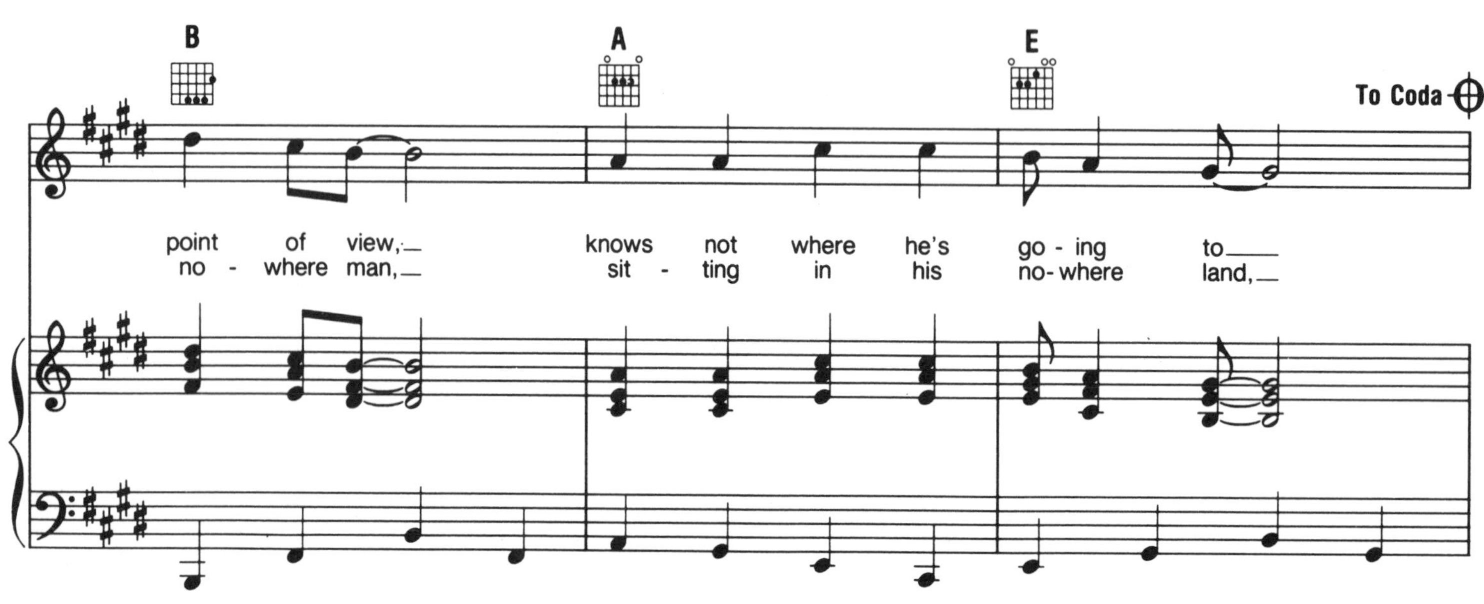
B
A
E
To Coda
point of view,
no - where man,
knows not where he's go - ing to
sit - ting in his no- where land,

A
Am
1 E
Is - n't he a bit like you and me?
2 E
D.S. al Coda
me?
No - where man,
CODA
A
Am
E
Mak - ing all his no - where plans for no - bod - y,
A
Am
E
Mak - ing all his no - where plans for no - bod - y.

OB-LA-DI, OB-LA-DA

Words and Music by
JOHN LENNON and PAUL McCARTNEY

E♭
B♭
like your face," and Mol - ly says this as she
at the door and as he gives it to her
F7
B♭
takes him by the hand:
she be - gins to sing:
Ob - la - di Ob - la - da
Dm
Gm
B♭
life goes on bra la la how the
F7
B♭
life goes on. Ob - la - di Ob - la - da

Dm
Gm
B♭
life goes on
bra
la
la how their
F7
B♭
1
2
life goes on.
E♭
In a cou-ple of years they have built a home sweet home.
B♭
Cm/B♭
B♭
B♭9

E♭
With a cou-ple of kids run - ning in the yard of
B♭
F7
Des - mond and Mol - ly Jones.
B♭
F7
Hap - py ev - er af - ter in the mar - ket place; Des -
Hap - py ev - er af - ter in the mar - ket place; Mol -
B♭
- mond lets the chil - dren lend a hand. Mol -
- ly lets the chil - dren lend a hand. Des -

E♭
-ly stays at home and does her pret - ty face
-mond stays at home and does his pret - ty face
B♭
F7
B♭
and in the eve - ning she still sings it with the band;
and in the eve - ning she's a sing - er with the band.
Dm
Ob - la - di Ob - la - da life goes on bra
Gm
B♭
F7
B♭
la la how the life goes on.

Dm
Ob - la - di Ob - la - da life goes on bra
Gm
Bb
F7
1 Bb
la la how the life goes on.
2 Gm
And if you want some fun
F7
Bb
take ob - la - di - bla - da.

OH! DARLING

Words and Music by
JOHN LENNON and PAUL McCARTNEY

1
A
D
A
E
harm.
Oh,
2
A
D
A
A7
lone.
When you
D
F7
told me
you did-n't need me an-y-more.
Well you
A
know I near - ly broke down
and cried.
When you

B7
told me
you did - n't need me an - y - more,
Well you
E7
F7-5
E7
E+
know, I near - ly fell down and died.
Oh,
A
E
dar - ling, if you leave me,
dar - ling, please be - lieve me,
F♯m
D
I'll nev - er make it a - lone;
I'll nev - er let you down.
(Spoken) Oh, believe me darling
Be -

Bm7
E7
1
Bm7
E7
lieve me when I tell you
lieve me when I tell you
I'll nev - er do you no
A
D
A
A7
harm.
(Spoken) Believe me, darling
When you
2
Bm7
E7
A
D
A
B♭7
A7
I'll nev - er do you no harm.

OLD BROWN SHOE

Moderately bright shuffle

Words and Music by
GEORGE HARRISON

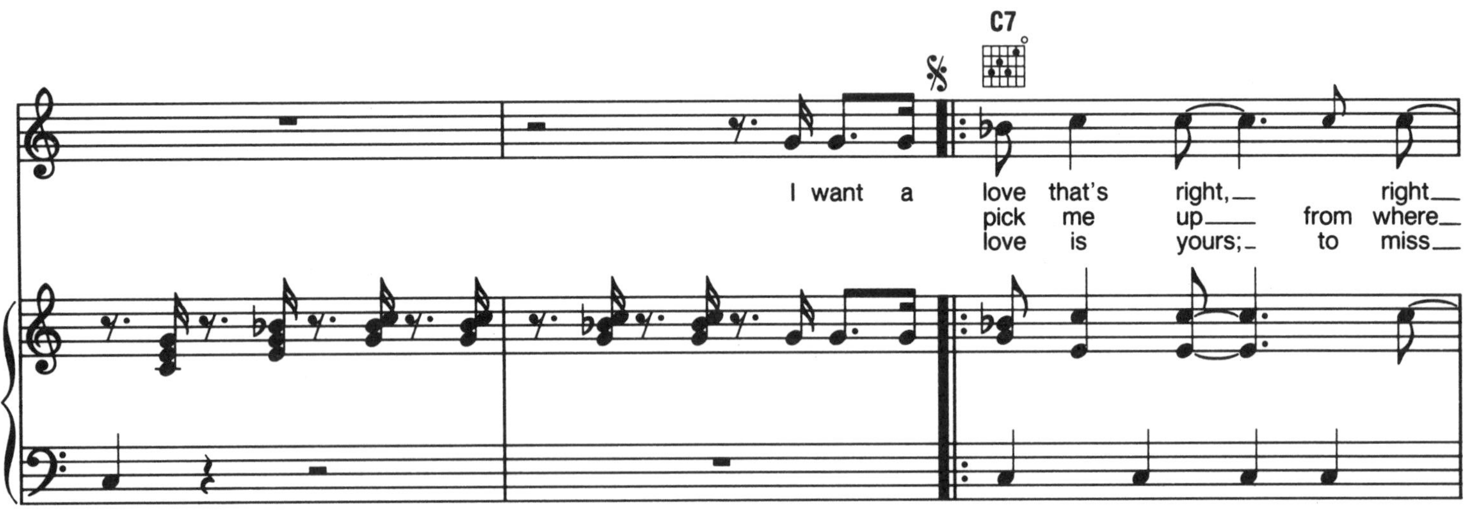

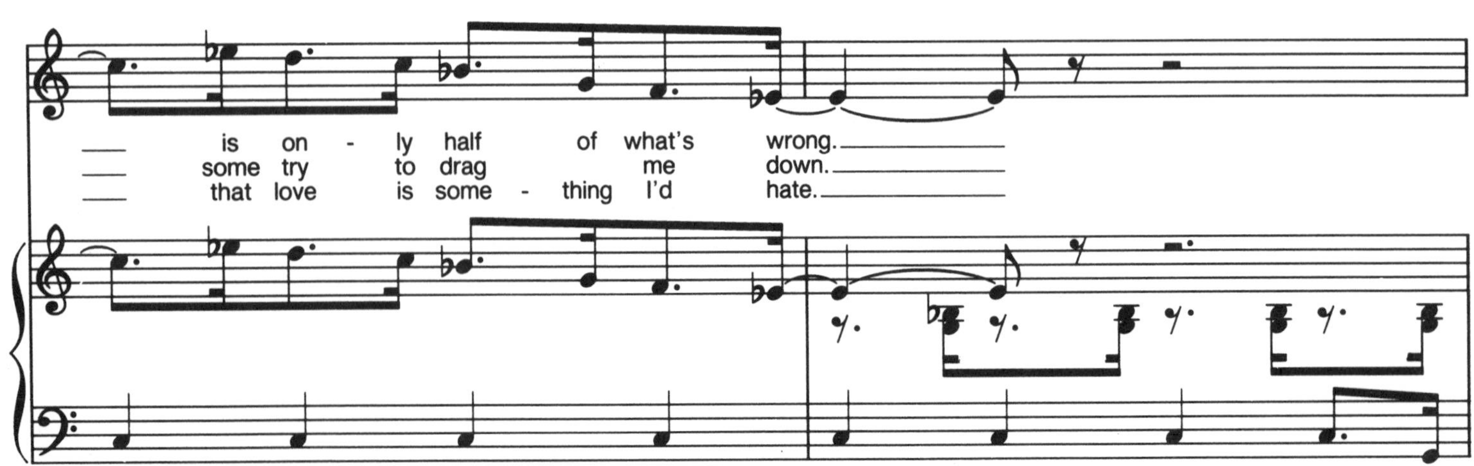

Dm7
I want a short - haired girl who
And when I see your smile re -
I'll make an ear - ly start, I'm

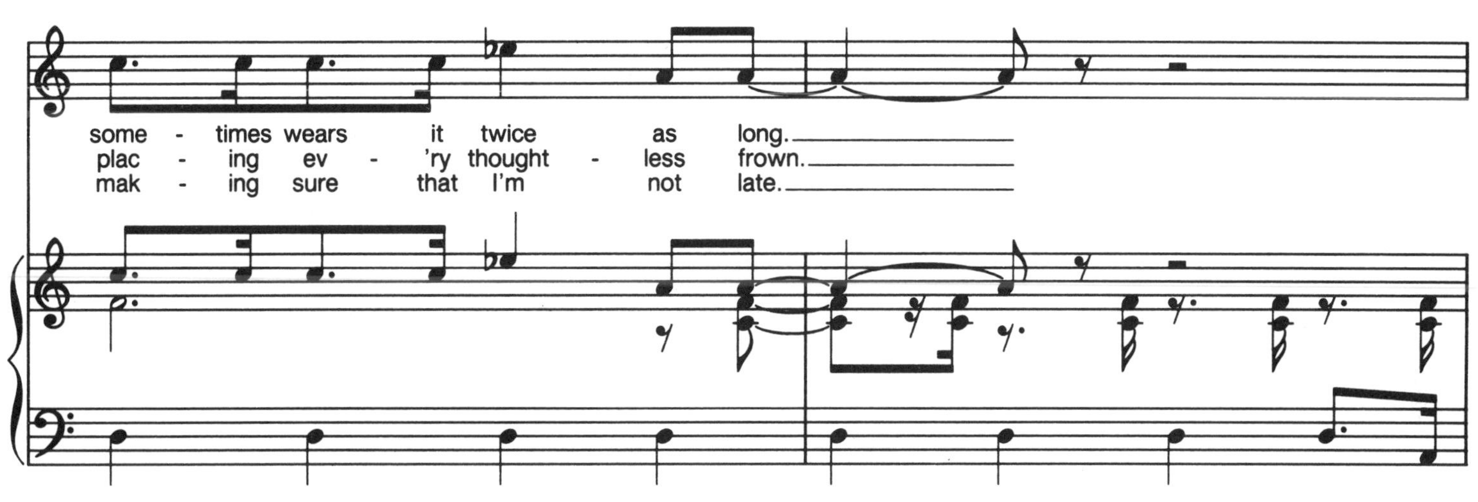
some - times wears it twice as long.
plac - ing ev - 'ry thought - less frown.
mak - ing sure that I'm not late.

F
Now I'm step - pin' out this old
Got me es - cap - ing from
For your sweet top lip I'm in

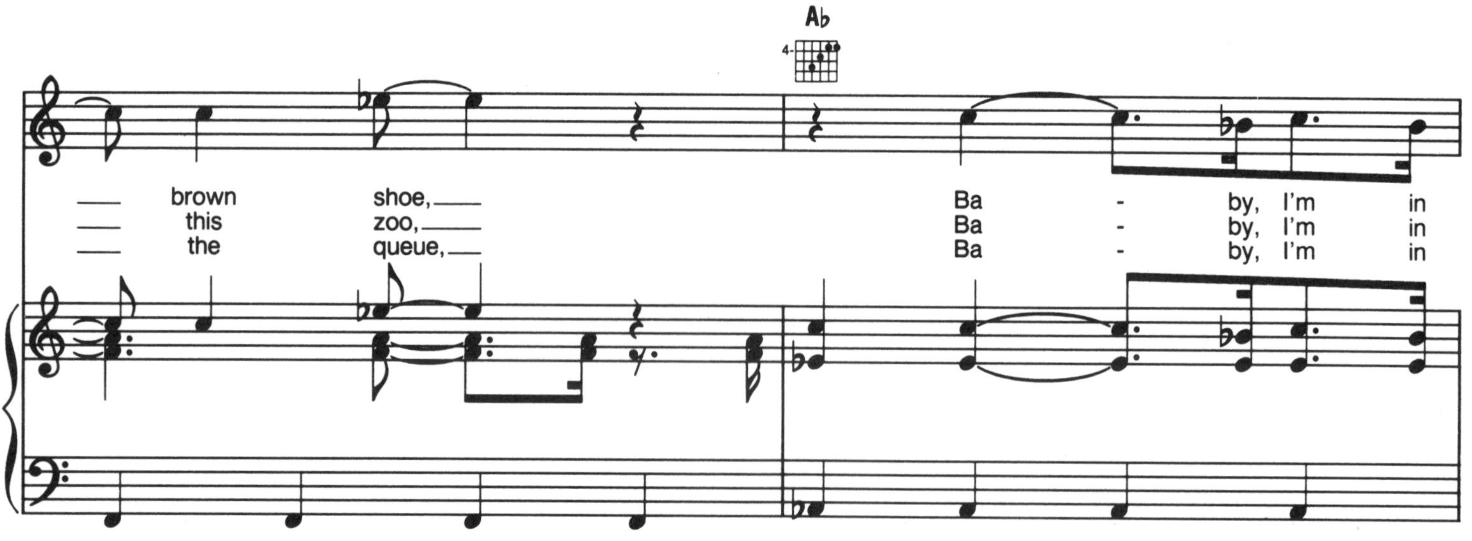
A♭
brown shoe, Ba - by, I'm in
this zoo, Ba - by, I'm in
the queue, Ba - by, I'm in

F
love with you. I'm so glad you came here, it won't
love with you. I'm so glad you came here, it won't
love with you. I'm so glad you came here, it won't

E7
Am
To Coda
be the same now. I'm tell - ing you.
be the same now, when I'm with you.
be the same now, when I'm with you.

1
C7
Though you
2 Am
G
If I grow up I'll
be a sing - er,
wear - ing rings on
F7
G
ev - 'ry fin - ger,
Not wor - ry - ing what they
3

F7
— or you'll say.
I'll live and love and may - be some - day,
F#dim7
G7
Who knows, ba - by? You may com - fort me.
C7
Hey!
Dm7

F
Ab
F
E7
Am
G
I may ap - pear to

be im - per - fect, my love is some - thing
F7
G
you can't re - ject. I'm chang - ing fast - er than
the weath - er, If you and me should
F7
F♯dim7
get to - geth - er, Who knows, ba - by?

G7
D.S. al Coda
you may com - fort me.
I know my
CODA
Am
F
I'm so glad you came here, it won't
E7
Am
be the same now, when I'm with you.
C7
Repeat and Fade

ONE AFTER 909

Words and Music by
JOHN LENNON and PAUL McCARTNEY

trav - el - lin' on that line."
on - ly fool - in' round with me."
trav - el - lin' on that line."
I said,
C7
no chord
C7
no chord
F7
"Move o - ver!" once,
"Move o - ver!" twice,
"Come on, ba - by, don't be
C7
To Coda
G7
cold as ice!"
She said she's trav - 'llin' on the one af - ter Nine - O - Nine.
C7
1
2
2. I

F7
C7
Picked up my bags,
run to the sta -
D7
- tion.
Rail - man said,
"You got the
G7
F7
wrong lo - ca - tion."
Picked up my bags,
C7
run right home.

D7
G7
Then I find— I've got the num-ber wrong! Well,
3
C7
Yeah.
F7

C7
G7
C7
D.S. al Coda
CODA
G7
one af - ter Nine - O, -
C7
G7
C7
she said she's trav - 'llin' on the one af - ter Nine - O, - she said she's trav - 'llin' on the
G7
C7
F
Ab7
C7
one af - ter Nine - O - Nine.

PENNY LANE

Words and Music by JOHN LENNON and PAUL McCARTNEY

C Am7 Dm7 G7sus C Am

corner is a banker with a motorcar; The little children laugh at him behind his
Lane: the barber shaves another customer, We see the banker sitting waiting for a

Cm7 Am7-5 A♭maj7

back. And the banker never wears a mac in the pour-
trim. And then the fireman rushes in from the pour-

G7sus G7 F B♭

-ing rain, very strange! Penny Lane is in my ears
-ing rain, very strange! Penny Lane is in my ears

B♭/D E♭ B♭

and in my eyes, wet beneath the blue
and in my eyes, there beneath the blue

Bb/D
Eb
To Coda
G
sub - ur - ban skies I sit. And mean - while back in Pen-ny Lane
sub - ur - ban skies I sit. And
C
Am
Dm7
G7sus
there is a fire-man with an hour glass, And in his pock - et is a por-trait of the
Cm7
Am7-5
Abmaj7
Queen. He likes to keep his fire en-gine clean; It's a clean
G7sus
G7
ma-chine!

Dm7
G
C
Am
Cm
Am7-5
A♭maj7
G7sus
F
Pen-ny Lane
B♭
B♭/D
E♭
is in my ears and in my eyes
B♭
B♭/D
Full of fish and fin - ger pies

E♭
G
D.S. al Coda
CODA
G
in sum - mer. Mean - while back be - hind the
mean - while back... Pen - ny Lane
C
C/E
F
is in my ears and in my eyes.
C
C/E
There be - neath the blue sub - ur - ban skies
F
C
Pen - ny Lane.

ONLY A NORTHERN SONG

Words and Music by
GEORGE HARRISON

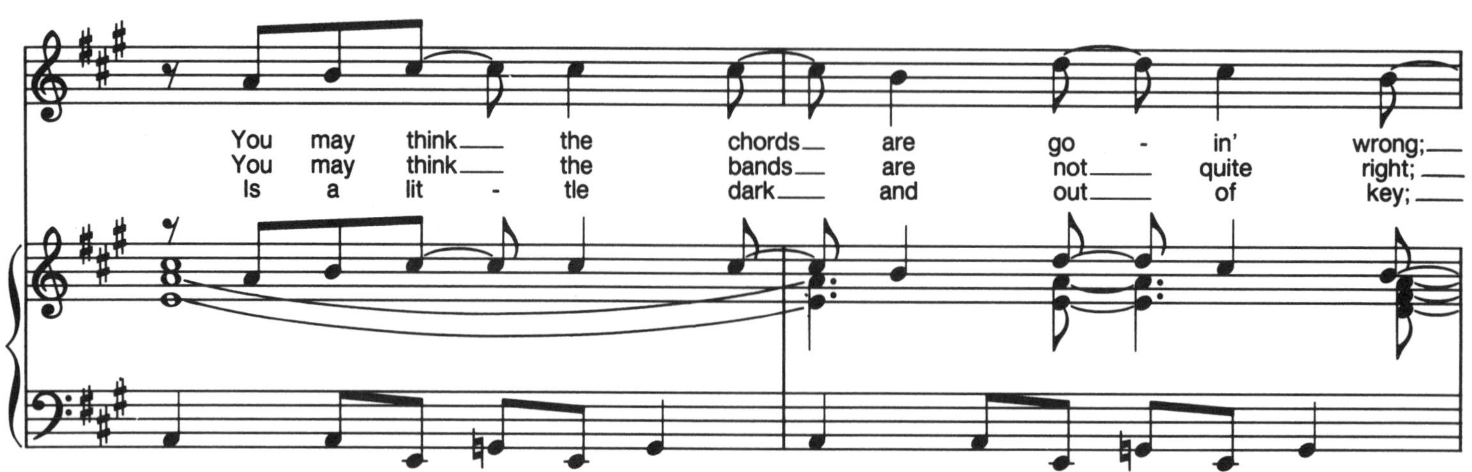

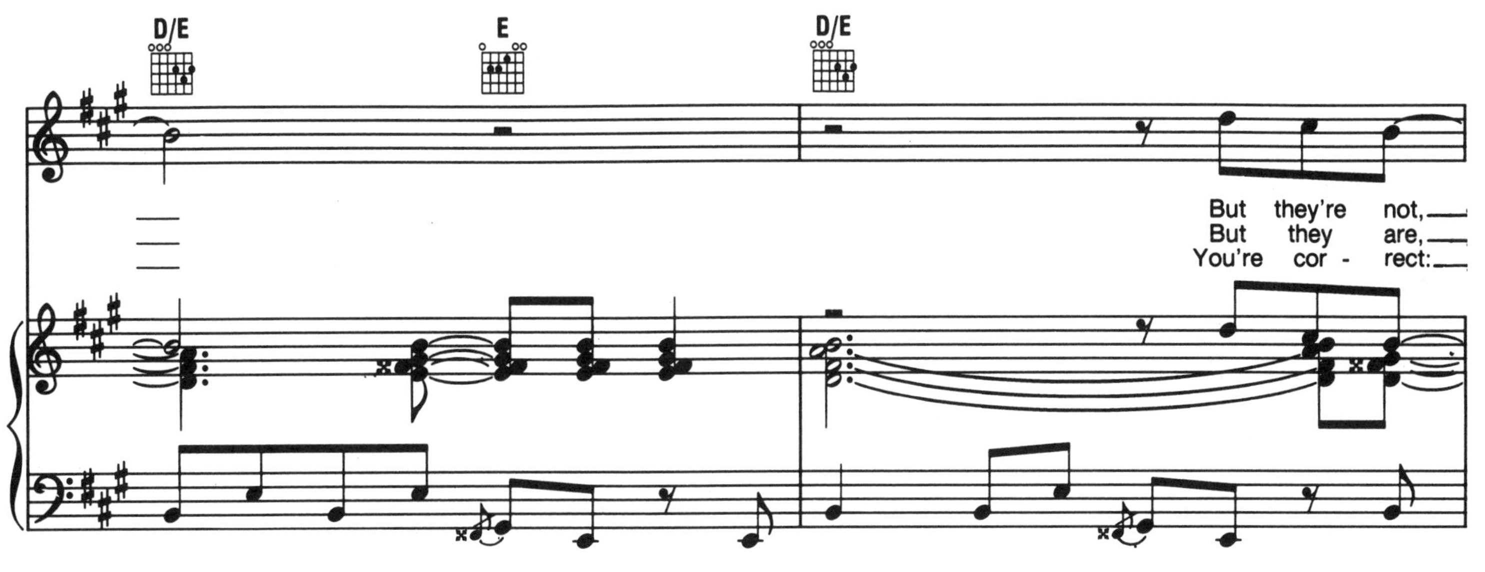
D/E
E
D/E
But they're not,
But they are,
You're cor - rect:

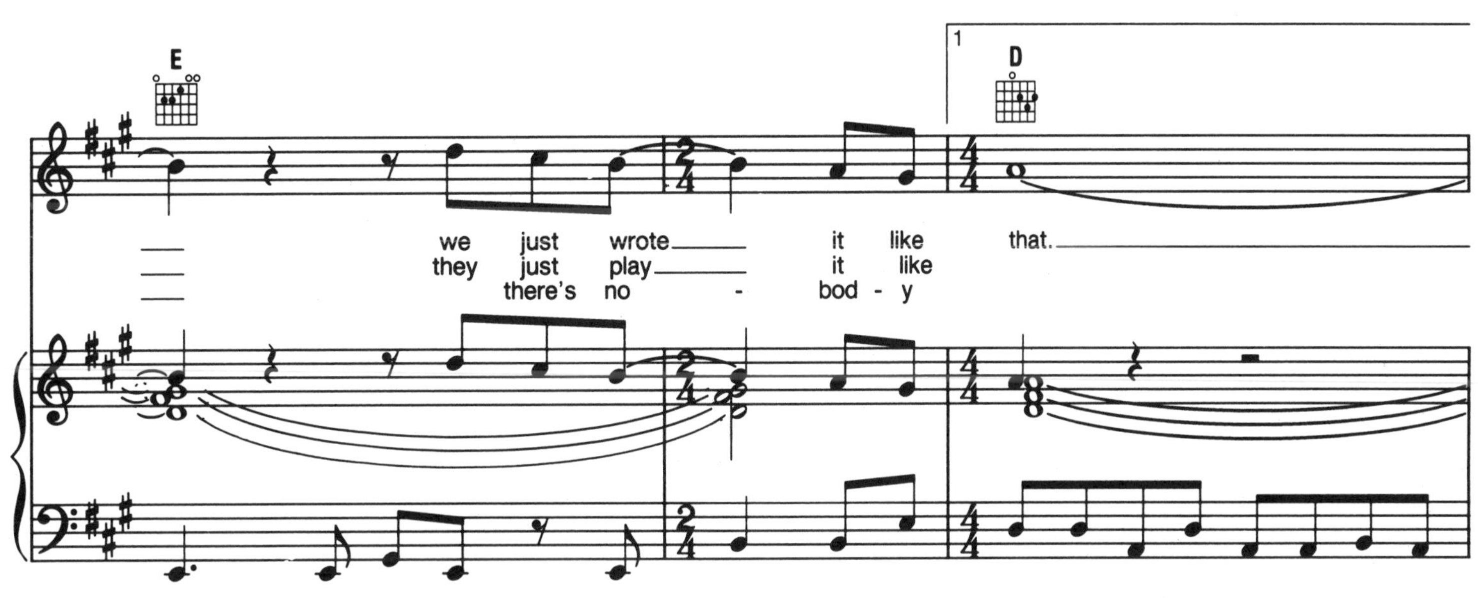
E
1
D
we just wrote it like that.
they just play it like
there's no - bod - y

2,3
D
that.
there.
It

E
Bm
G
C♯7
does - n't real - ly mat - ter what chords I play, what
does - n't real - ly mat - ter what clothes I wear, or
F♯7
Bm
words I say or time of day it
how I fare, or if my hair is
F♯7
D
A
To Coda
is
brown
As it's on - ly a North - ern
When it's on - ly a North - ern
And I told you there's no one
1
Esus
A
Song.

Esus
D
It
2
Esus
D.S. al Coda
Song.
CODA
E
there.

P.S. I LOVE YOU

Words and Music by
JOHN LENNON and PAUL McCARTNEY

D
D/A
A7
D
always be in love with you.
D
Em7
D
Treasure these few words till we're together, Keep
A7
Bm7
A
A7
all my love forever, P. S. I love
B♭
C7
D
you. you, you, you.

D
Em7
1. 3. I'll be com - ing home a - gain to
2. Treas - ure these few words till we're to -
D
A7
Bm7
you love and till the day I do love,
geth - er, keep all my love for - ev - er,
A
A7
B♭
To Coda
C7
P. S. I love you, you, you,
D
G
D
you.
As I write this let - ter
As I write this let - ter, oh,

G
D
G
send my love to you, re - mem - ber that I'll
send my love to you, you know I want you to re - mem - ber that I'll
D
D/A
A7
1 D
al - ways___ be in love with___ you.
al - ways,___ yeah,___ be in love with___
2 D
D.S. al Coda
you.
CODA
D
B♭
C7
you,___ you,___ you,___
D
B♭
C7
D
you,___ I love you.___

PAPERBACK WRITER

Words and Music by
JOHN LENNON and PAUL McCARTNEY

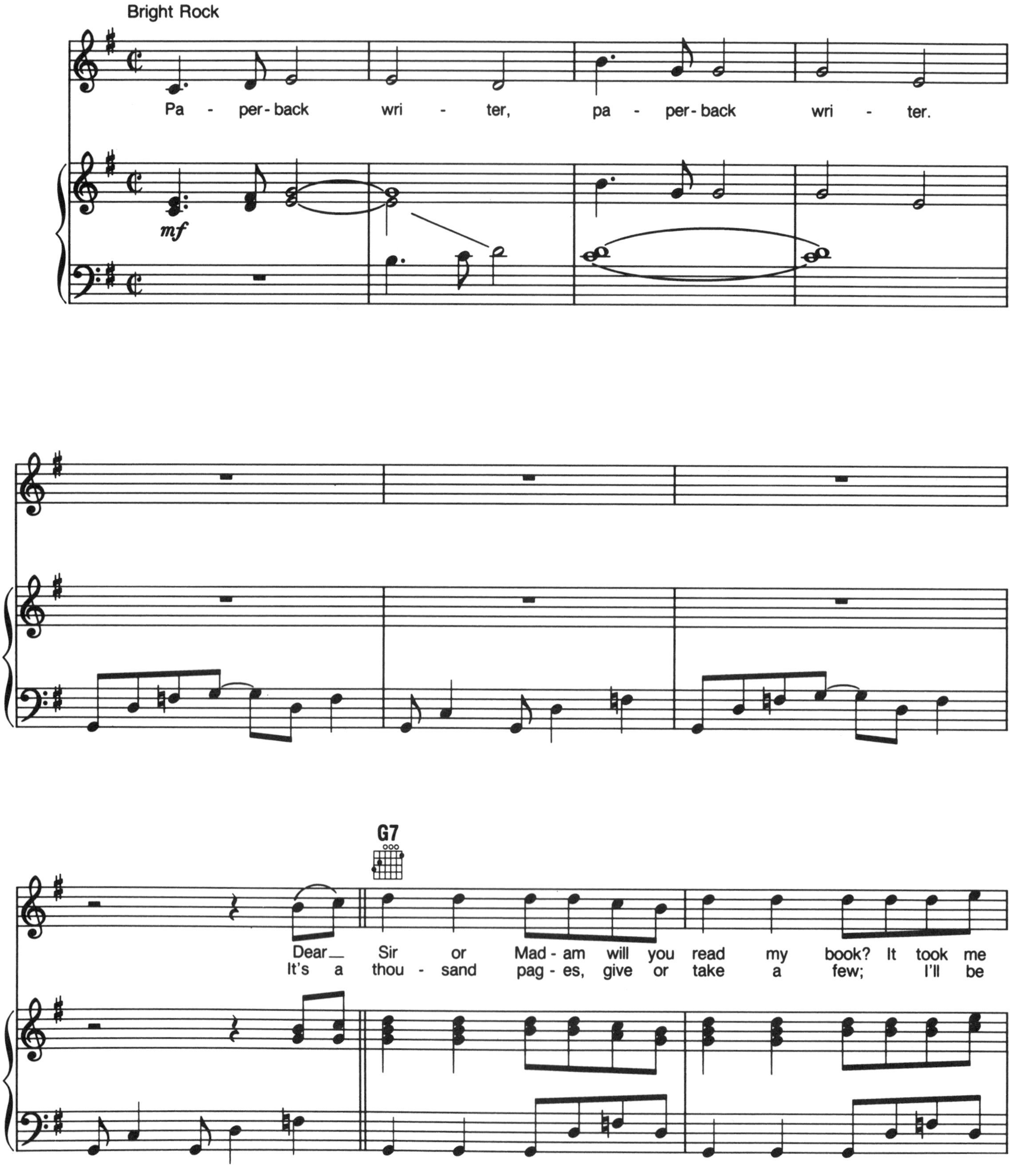

Bright Rock
Pa - per-back wri - ter, pa - per-back wri - ter.
mf
G7
Dear Sir or Mad - am will you read my book? It took me
It's a thou - sand pag - es, give or take a few; I'll be

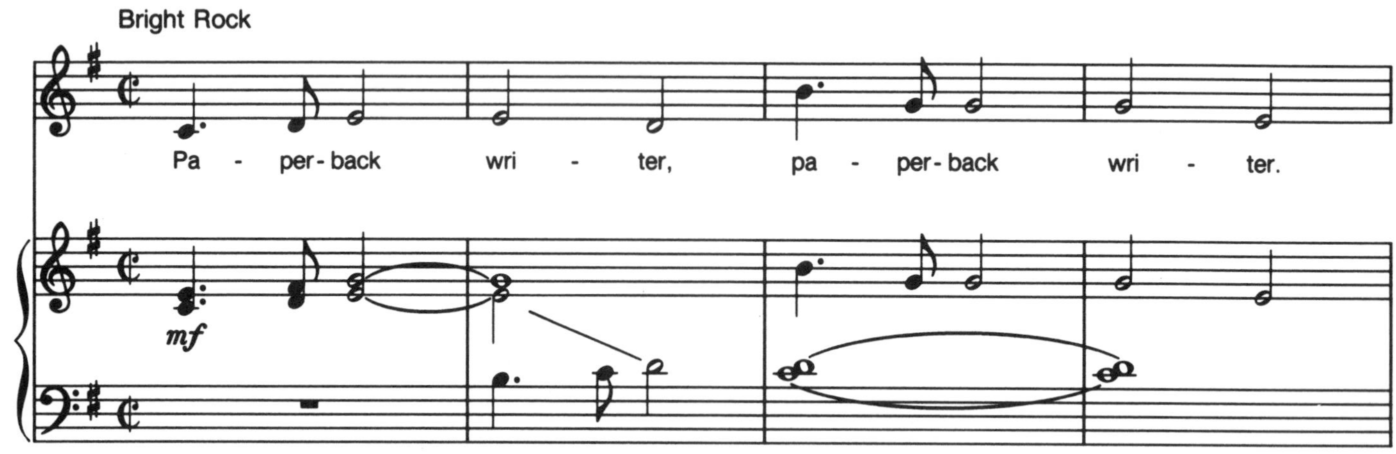

years to write, will you take a look? It's based on a nov - el by a
writ - ing more in a week or two. I can make it long - er if you
man named Lear and I need a job so I
like the style, I can change it 'round and I
C
want to be a pa - per - back writ - er, pa - per - back
want to be a pa - per - back writ - er, pa - per - back
G7
writ - er. It's the dir - ty sto - ry of a
writ - er. If you real - ly like it you can

dirt - y man, and his cling - ing wife doesn't un-der-stand. His
have the rights, it could make a mil - lion for you o-ver-night. If you
son is work - ing for the Dai - ly Mail; It's a
must re - turn it you can send it here, But I
C
stead - y job but he wants to be a pa-per-back writ - er,
need a break and I want to be a pa-per-back writ - er,
G7
pa - per-back writ - er.
pa - per-back writ - er.

no chord
Pa - per - back writ - er, pa - per - back
writ - er.
G7
Pa - per - back
writ - er.
Repeat and Fade

PIGGIES

Words and Music by
GEORGE HARRISON

E♭ Fm7 F♯dim7 E♭/G A♭ E♭
1
A♭ E♭
play a - round in.
play a - round in.
2
A♭ C7 B♭m C7 D♭ A♭
In their sties with all their back-ing, they don't care what
E♭
goes on a - round,
B♭m C7 D♭ E♭
In their eyes there's some-thing lack-ing, What they need's a damn good whack-ing!

Eb7
Ab
Eb7
Ab
Eb
Ab
Eb7
Fm
Bb
Fm
Bb
Eb
Db/F
F#dim7
Eb/G
Ab
Eb
Ab
Eb

Ab
Eb
Ab
Eb
Ev - 'ry - where there's lots of pig-gies liv - ing pig - gy lives,
Ab
Eb
Fm
Bb
Fm
Bb
You can see them out for din-ner with their pig-gy wives Clutch-ing forks and knives to
Eb
Fm7
F#dim7
Eb/G
Ab
Eb
Abm
Eb
eat their ba - con.
Abm
Eb7
Bb7
Eb
A
E
(Spoken): One more time

PLEASE PLEASE ME

F#m
C#m
A
on (Come on)
Come on (Come on)
Come on, (Come on)
Please,
E
To Coda
A
B7
E
please me, wo yeah, like I please you.
1
Amaj9
B
2
E
A
I don't want to sound com - plain - ing
B7
E
A
E
but you know there's al - ways rain in my heart.
(in my heart).

A B7 E
I do all the pleas-ing with you, it's so hard to rea-son with you, wo
A B7 E Amaj9 B
D.S. al Coda
yeah, why do you make me blue?
CODA
A B7 E A B7
yeah, like I please you, wo yeah, like I please
E G C B7 E
you.

PLEASE MR. POSTMAN

Words and Music by BRIAN HOLLAND, ROBERT BATEMAN, FREDDIE GORMAN, GEORGIA DOBBINS and WILLIAM GARRETT

D
I've been a - wait - ing a long, long time
Mis - ter Po - wo - wost - man, oh,
Mis - ter Po - wo - wost - man, oh,
E
Since I heard from that girl of mine.
yeah.
yeah.
A
There must be some word to - day
So man - y days you've passed me by,
F♯m
From my girl - friend so far a - way.
See the tears stand - in' in my eyes.

D
E
To Coda
Please, Mis - ter Post - man, look and see if there's a let - ter, a
You did - n't stop to make me feel bet - ter by leav - ing me a
A
let - ter for me. I've been stand - in' here wait - ing Mis - ter Post - man,
F#m
D
so pa - tient - ly For just a card,
E
D.S. al Coda
or just a let - ter say - ing she's re - turn - ing home to me. Then Mis - ter

CODA
E
A
Mis - ter Post - man, look
card or a let - ter, Mis - ter Post - man,
and see,
F#m
Is there a let - ter in your bag for me?
D
E
I've been wait - ing for such a long time
Since I heard from that
A
girl - friend of mine. You got - ta wait a min - ute, wait a min - ute, oh yeah.

F#m
Wait a min - ute, wait a min - ute, oh yeah,
You got - ta
Mist - ter
You got - ta
D
wait a min - ute, wait a min - ute, oh yeah.
Po - wo - wost - man, oh yeah. De -
wait a min - ute, wait a min - ute, oh yeah. Got - ta
1
E
Check it and see one more time for me. You got - ta
2
E
liv - er the let - ter, the
soon - er the bet - You got - ta
3
E
wait a min - ute, wait a min - ute, oh yeah. You got - ta
Repeat and Fade

RAIN

Words and Music by
JOHN LENNON and PAUL McCARTNEY

2
G
shines.
Rain
C(add9)
I don't mind
G
Shine,
C(add9)
The wea - ther's fine.

G
I can show you that
Can you hear me that
C D G C D
when it starts to rain ev - 'ry - thing's the
when it rains and shines it's just a state of
G C
same. I can show you. I can
mind. Can you hear me? Can you
G
show you.
hear me?
1
2

ROCKY RACCOON

Am7
D7sus
Rock - y Rac - coon checked in - to his room
she and her man who called him - self Dan
L.H.
D7
G7
were on - ly to find Gid - eon's Bi -
in the next room at the hoe -
C
C/B
Am7
- ble. Rock - y had come e -
- down. Rock - y burst in and
D7sus
D7
G7
quipped with a gun to shoot off the legs
grin - ning a grin, He said, "Dan - ny boy, this

C
C/B
of his ri - val.
His
is a show - down."
But
Am7
D7sus
D7
ri - val it seems had bro - ken his dreams by
Dan - iel was hot, he drew first and shot and
G7
C
C/B
steal - ing the girl of his fan - cy.
Her
Rock - y col - lapsed in the cor - ner.
1
Am7
D7
name was Ma - gill, And she called her - self Lil, but

G7
C
C/B
ev - 'ry - one knew her as Nan - cy.
Now
2 Barrelhouse style
played as
3
Am7
D7
G7
C
C/B
Am7
Now the doc - tor came in

D7sus
D7
stink - ing of gin and pro -
G7
C
C/B
ceed - ed to lie on the ta - ble.
He said,
Am7
D7sus
"Rock - y, you met your match,"
And Rock - y said, "Doc, it's on - ly a scratch,
D7
G7
And I'll be bet - ter, I'll be bet - ter Doc, as soon as I am

C
C/B
Am7
a - ble."
Now Rock - y Rac - coon,
he fell
D7
G7
back in his room
on - ly to find
C
C/B
Am7
Gid - eon's Bi - ble.
Gid - eon checked out
D7sus
D7
and he left it no doubt
to

G7
C
C/B
help with good Rock - y's re - vi - val.
Am7
Barrelhouse style (played as 3)
D7
G7
1
C
C/B
2
C

REVOLUTION

Words and Music by
JOHN LENNON and PAUL McCARTNEY

C
3
to change the world. You
to see the plan. You
to change your head. You

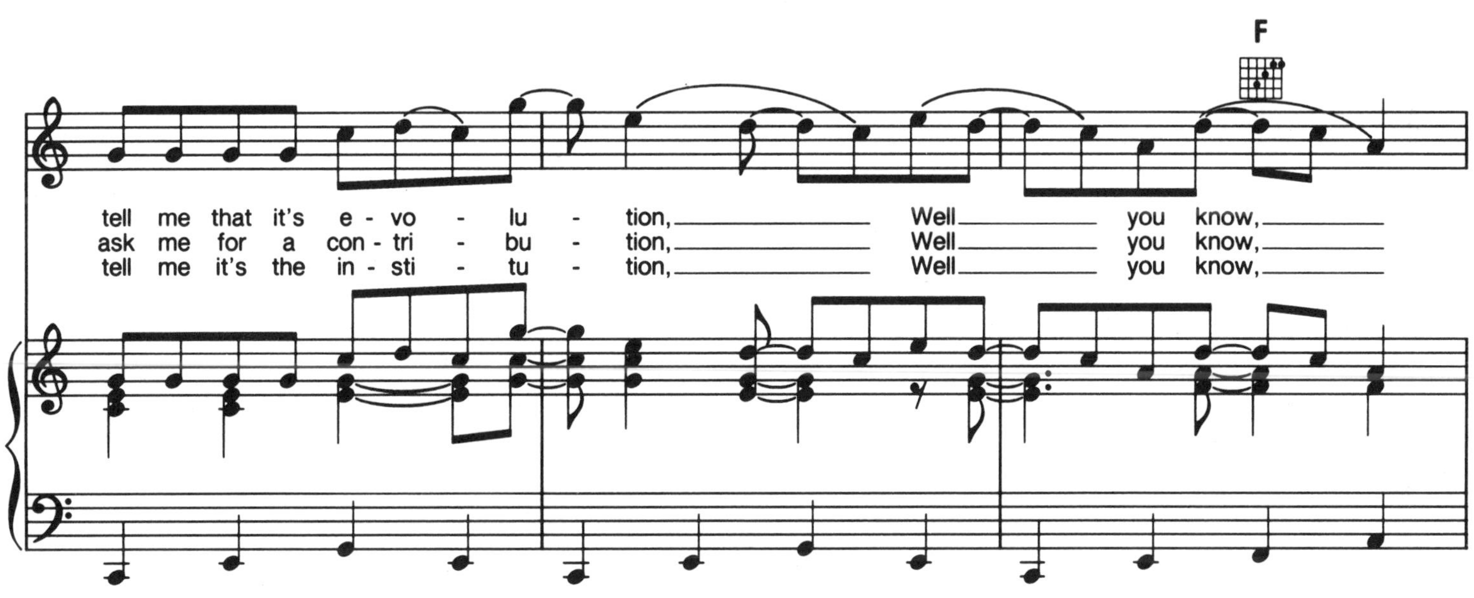
F
tell me that it's e - vo - lu - tion, Well you know,
ask me for a con - tri - bu - tion, Well you know,
tell me it's the in - sti - tu - tion, Well you know,

G7
We all want to change the world.
We're all do - ing what we can.
You better free your mind in - stead.
3

Dm
G6
But when you talk a - bout de - struc - tion,
But if you want money for people with minds that hate,
But if you go carry - ing pictures of Chair - man Mao,
Dm
B♭
C
A
Don't you know that you can count me out.
All I can tell you is, "Brother you have to wait."
You ain't going to make it with any - one an - y - how.
G11
C
F6
Don't you know it's gon - na be al - right,
C
F6
C
al - right,
al - right.

F6
G11
1,2
C
G11
You
You
3
C
G7
C
F
Al - right,
al - right,
al - right,
C
F
C
al - right,
al - right,
al - right,
F
G7
C
al - right,
al - right.

RUN FOR YOUR LIFE

Bm
lit - tle girl, or I (you) won't know where I am.
life try - in' just to make you toe the line.
- mined and I'd rath - er see you dead.
E
You'd bet - ter run for your life if you can, lit - tle girl;
Bm
E
Hide your head in the sand lit - tle girl,
Bm
G6
F#7
Bm
To Coda
Catch you with an - oth - er man, that's the end - a, lit - tle

1,3
D
girl.
2
Well, you
I'd
girl.
D7
3
G7

D7
A7
D
Am7
D.S. al Coda
CODA
Bm
D7
girl.
Repeat and Fade
No, no, no.

SAVOY TRUFFLE

Words and Music by
GEORGE HARRISON

A
G
Cof - fee des - sert,
Co - co - nut fudge
B7
yes, you know it's good news,
real - ly blows down those blues,
Em
C/E
But you'll have to have them all pulled out
Em6
C/E
Cmaj7
To Coda
G
af - ter the Sav - oy Truf - fle.

1
E7
Cool cher - ry
2
Em
A
Asus
A
You might not feel it now,
when the pain cuts through, you're gon - na
G
B
Em
know, and how.
The sweat is gon - na fill your head;
A
Asus
A
G
B
When it be - comes too much
you'll shout a - loud.

E
F♯
A
G
B7
But you'll

Em
C/E
Em6
C/E
have to have them all pulled out after the Sav - oy
Cmaj7
G
Truf - fle.
You
Em
A
know that what you eat you are,
but what is
Asus
A
G
B
sweet now turns so sour,
We

Em
A
all know 'Ob - la - di - bla - da',
but can you
Asus
A
G
B
E7
D.S. al Coda
show me where you are?
Cream tan - ger - ine,
CODA
G
Em
C/E
Yes, you'll have to have them all pulled out
Em6
C/E
Cmaj7
G
af - ter the Sav - oy Truf - fle.

SEXY SADIE

Words and Music by
JOHN LENNON and PAUL McCARTNEY

F D G Am
Sa - die, Oh you broke the rules. One sun - ny day, the world was wait - ing for a
You gave her ev - 'ry - thing you owned just to sit at her
Bm C G Am Bm C
lov - er; She came a - long to turn on ev - 'ry - one. Sex - y Sa -
ta - ble; Just as smile would light - en ev - 'ry - thing. Sex - y Sa -
A7 Ab7 To Coda G F#
die, the great - est of them all. Sex - y Sa - die,
die, the lat - est and the great - est of them all.
Bm C D G F#
how did you know the world was wait - ing just for you,
you'll get yours yet, how - ev - er big you think you are,

C
D
G
F♯
the world was wait - ing just for you?
how-ev - er big you think you are.
Sex-y
1
F
D
2
F
D
D.S. al Coda
Sa - die, Oh how did you know?
Sa - die, Oh you'll get yours yet.
CODA
G
F♯
Bm
Sex-y Sa-die, she's the latest and the great-est of them all.
"Oo
C
D
G
F♯
C
D
Repeat and Fade

SGT. PEPPER'S LONELY HEARTS CLUB BAND

Words and Music by
JOHN LENNON and PAUL McCARTNEY

A7
C
may I in-tro-duce to you
the act you've known for all these years:
let me in-tro-duce to you
the one and on-ly Bil-ly Shears.
G
C
G
C7
Ser-geant Pep-per's Lone-ly Hearts Club Band.
F
C
D7
G
Bb
F
We're Ser-geant Pep-per's Lone-ly Hearts
We're Ser-geant Pep-per's Lone-ly Hearts

C G C G
Club Band, We hope you will en - joy the show
Club Band. We hope you have en - joyed the show.
B♭ F C G
Ser - geant Pep - per's Lone - ly Hearts Club Band, Sit
Ser - geant Pep - per's Lone - ly Hearts Club Band, We're
A7 D7 C G
back and let the eve - ning go.
sor - ry but it's time to go.
Ser - geant Pep - per's Lone - ly, Ser -
Ser - geant Pep - per's Lone - ly, Ser -
A7 C
- geant Pep - per's Lone - ly, Ser - geant Pep - per's Lone - ly Hearts
- geant Pep - per's Lone - ly, Ser - geant Pep - per's Lone - ly Hearts

C/D G
1 C F7
Club Band. It's won-der-ful to be here, it's cer-tain-ly a thrill, You're
Club Band.
C D7
such a love-ly au-di-ence, we'd like to take you home with us, we'd love to take you home. I don't
2 G B♭ F C G C
Ser-geant Pep-per's Lone-ly Hearts Club Band, We'd like to thank you once a-gain.
G B♭ F C G
Ser-geant Pep-per's one and on-ly Lone-ly Hearts Club Band, It's

A7
D7
C
G
get - ting ver - y near the end.
Ser - geant Pep - per's Lone - ly, Ser - geant Pep - per's Lone - ly, Ser - geant Pep - per's Lone - ly Hearts
Club
Band.
B♭

SHE LOVES YOU

Words and Music by
JOHN LENNON and PAUL McCARTNEY

Em
Bm
D
Well, I saw her yes - ter - day.
It's
G
Em
Bm
you she's think - ing of
And she told me what to
D
G6
say:
She says she loves you
and you know that can't be
Em
Cm6
bad.
Yes, she loves you
and you

D
know you should be glad.
She
G
Em
Bm
said you hurt her so,
know it's up to you,
She almost lost her
I think it's on-ly
D
G
Em
mind.
fair.
But now she says she knows
Pride can hurt you too
You're
A-
Bm
D
G6
not the hurt-ing kind.
pol-o-gize to her.
She says she
Be-cause she
loves you and you

Em
Cm6
know that can't be bad.
Yes, she loves you and you
D
Em
know you should be glad. oo!
She loves you, yeah,
A7
yeah, yeah,
She loves you, yeah, yeah, yeah. And with a
Cm6
D+
D7
1
G
love like that you know you should be glad.
You

G
Em
Cm6
With a love like that you
D+
D7
G
Em
Cm6
know you should be glad.
With a love like that you
D+
D7
G
Em
know you should be glad.
Yeah, yeah, yeah,
Yeah,
rit.
a tempo
C
G6
yeah, yeah,
Yeah, yeah, yeah, yeah!

SHE'S LEAVING HOME

Words and Music by
JOHN LENNON and PAUL McCARTNEY

B11
B9
Leav - ing the note that she hoped would say more She goes
Stand - ing a - lone at the top of the stairs She breaks

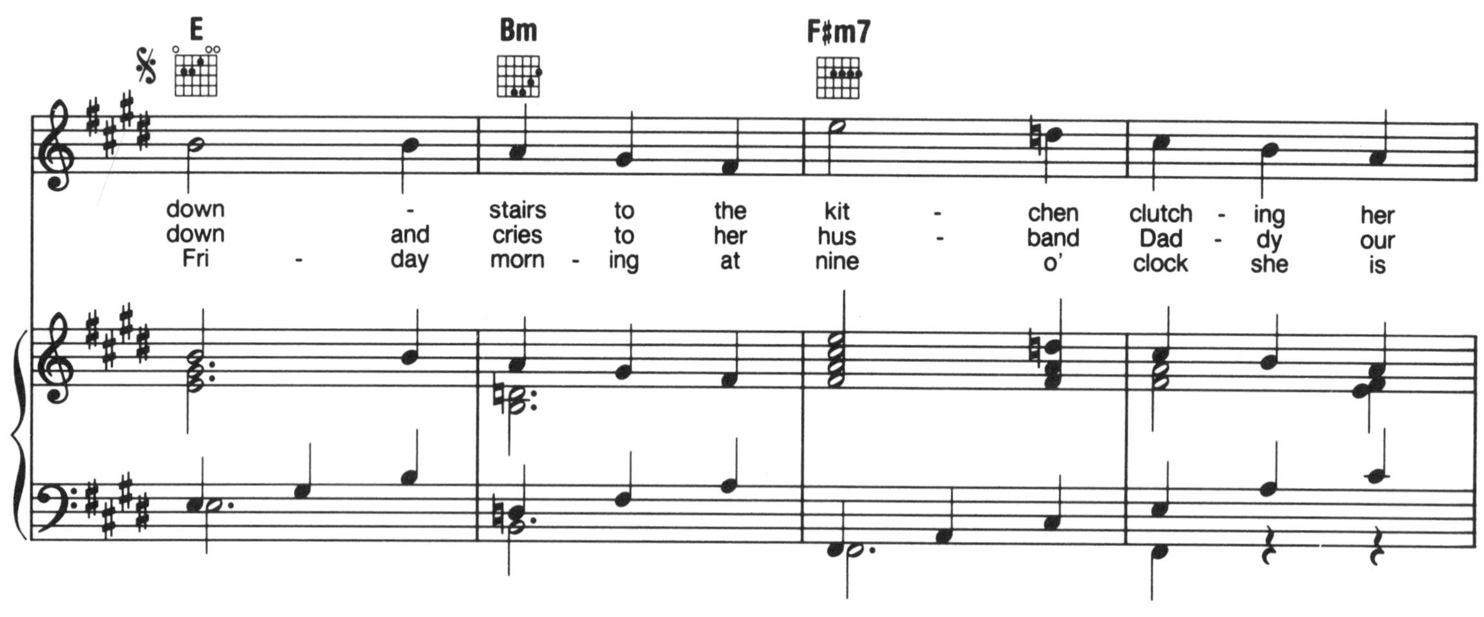
E
Bm
F#m7
down - stairs to the kit - chen clutch - ing her
down and cries to her hus - band Dad - dy our
Fri - day morn - ing at nine o' clock she is

C#m
F#7
hand - ker - chief
ba - by's gone
far a - way

B11
B9
Qui - et - ly turn - ing the back - door key
Why would she treat us so thought - less - ly
Wait - ing to keep the ap - point - ment she made

B11
B9
B7
Step - ping out - side she is free
How could she do this to me
Meet - ing a man from the mo - tor trade

E
She (We gave her most of our lives) is
She (We nev - er thought of our selves)
She (What did we do that was wrong) is

leav - ing (Sac - ri - ficed most of our lives)
leav - ing (Nev - er a thought for our selves)
hav - ing (We did - n't know it was wrong)

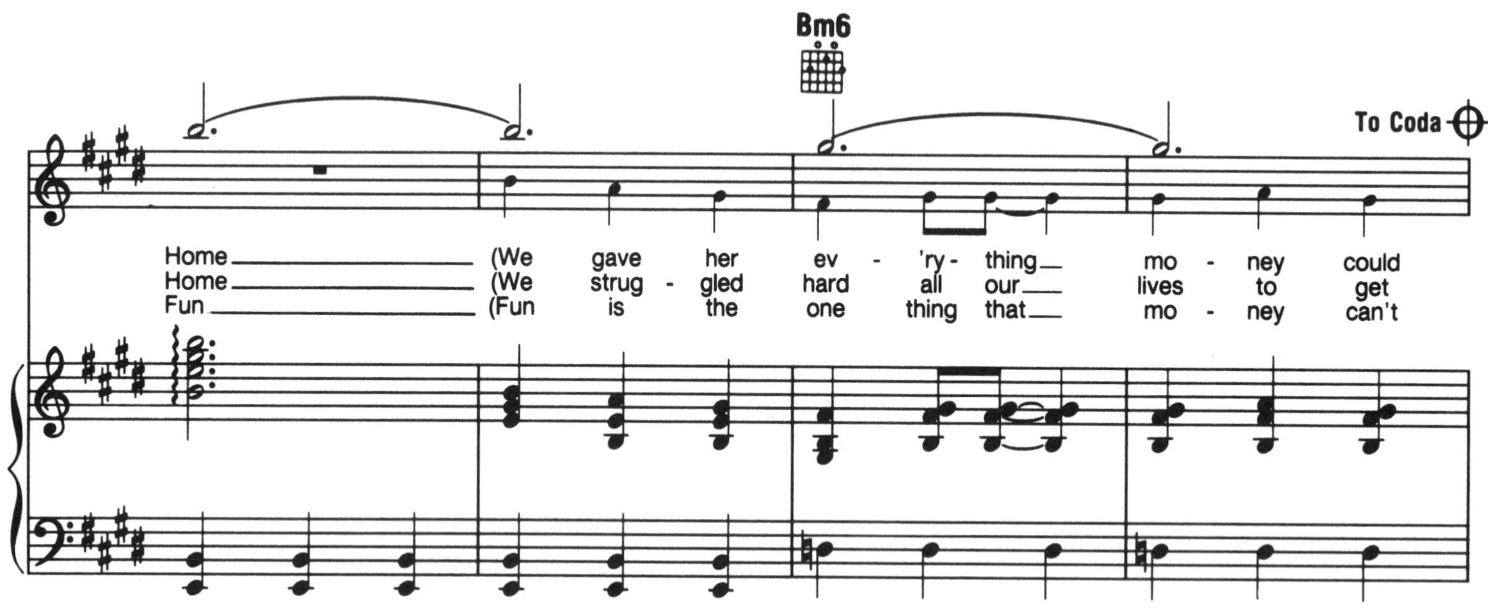
Bm6
To Coda
Home (We gave her ev - 'ry - thing mo - ney could
Home (We strug - gled hard all our lives to get
Fun (Fun is the one thing that mo - ney can't

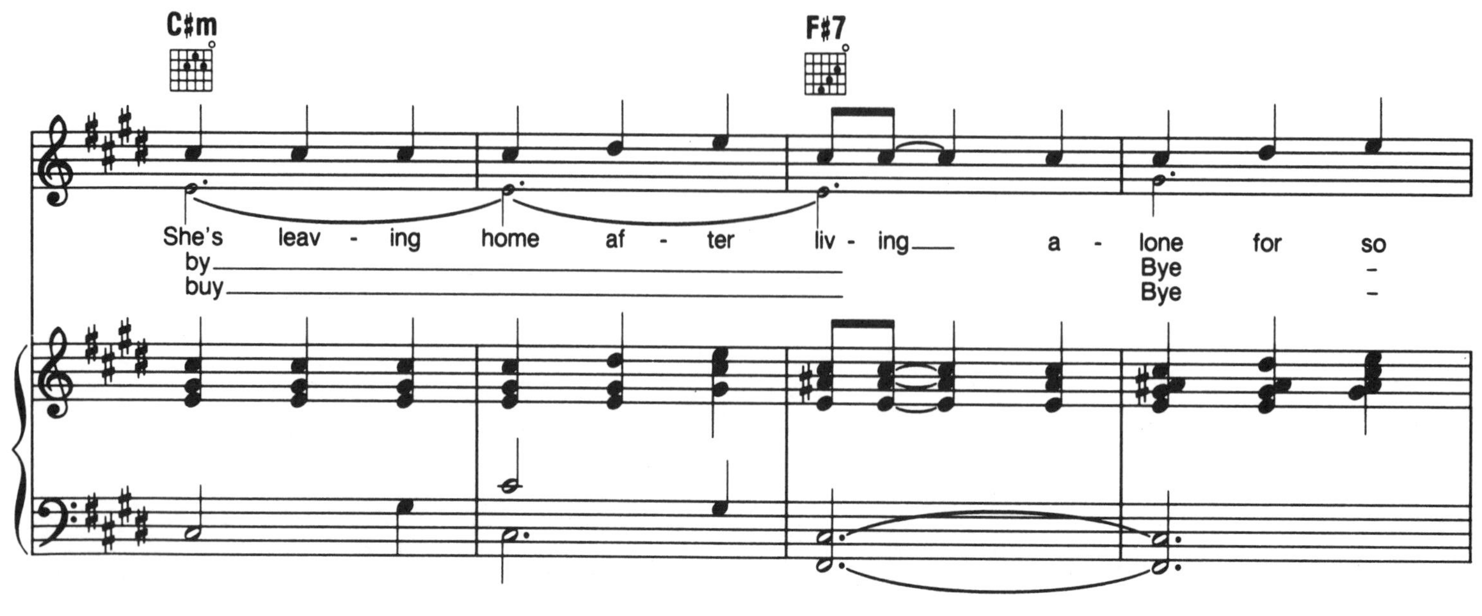
C♯m
F♯7
She's leav - ing home af - ter liv - ing a - lone for so
by Bye -
buy Bye -

C#m
1 F#9
2 F#9
D.S. al Coda
man - y years
bye)
bye)
CODA
C#m
F#7
C#m7
Some - thing in - side that was al - ways de - nied for so man - y years
buy Bye - bye)
F#7
C#m
She's leav - ing
F#7
A
E
home Bye - bye

SHE SAID SHE SAID

Words and Music by
JOHN LENNON and PAUL McCARTNEY

Eb
Bb
Ab
Eb
Bb
nev - er been born.
nev - er been born."
Bb
Ab
Bb
She said, "You don't un - der - stand what I said." I said,
Ab
Bb
Fm7
Bb7
"No, no no, you're wrong. When I was a boy
Eb
Bb7
ev - 'ry - thing was right,

Eb
Bb
Ab
ev - 'ry - thing was right." I said,
Eb
Bb
Ab(add9)
"E - ven though you know what you know,
Eb
Bb
Ab(add9)
3
I know that I'm read - y to leave,
3
Eb
Bb
Ab
'Cause you're mak - ing me feel like I've

E♭
B♭
A♭
E♭
B♭
nev - er been born." —
B♭7
She said,
(She said,)
"I know what it's
like to be dead,
("I know what it's like to be dead,)
I know what it
is to be sad."
(I know what it is to be sad.")
Repeat and Fade
"I know what it's

SHE'S A WOMAN

Words and Music by
JOHN LENNON and PAUL McCARTNEY

D7
On - ly ev - er has to give me love for - ev - er
She is hap - py just to hear me say that I will
A7
D7
and for - ev - er; My love don't give me pres - ents.
nev - er leave her; She don't give boys the eye.
A7
E7
Turn me on when I get lone - ly,
She will nev - er make me jeal - ous,
D7
A7
Peo - ple tell me that she's on - ly fool - in', I
Gives me all her time as well as lov - in', Don't

D7
To Coda
A7
1 E7
2 A7
know she is - n't.
ask me why.
C#m
F#7
C#m
She's a wom - an who un - der - stands;
She's a wom - an who
D
E
3 E7
A7
loves her man.
D7

A7
E7
D7
A7
C♯m
She's a wom - an who
F♯7
C♯m
D
E
D.S. al Coda
un - der - stands;
She's a wom - an who loves her man.
CODA
A7
Repeat and Fade
She's a wom - an,
She's a wom -

SLOW DOWN

Moderate rock and roll

Words and Music by
LARRY WILLIAMS

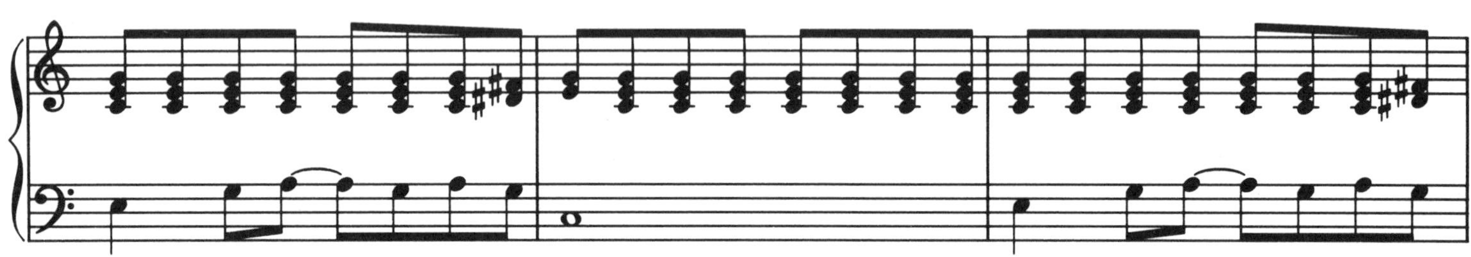

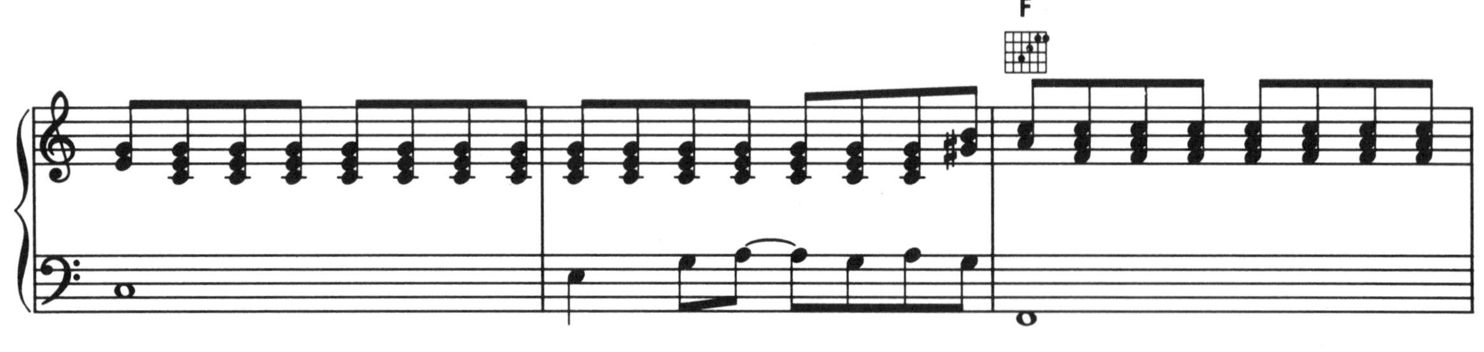

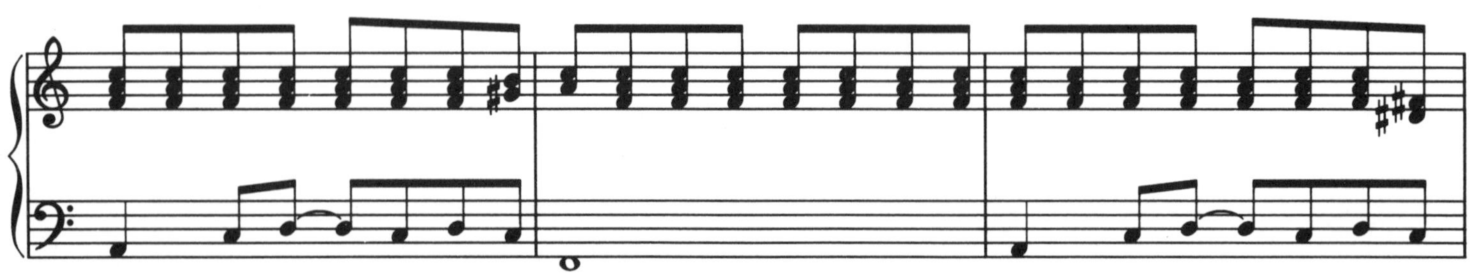

C

G

F
C

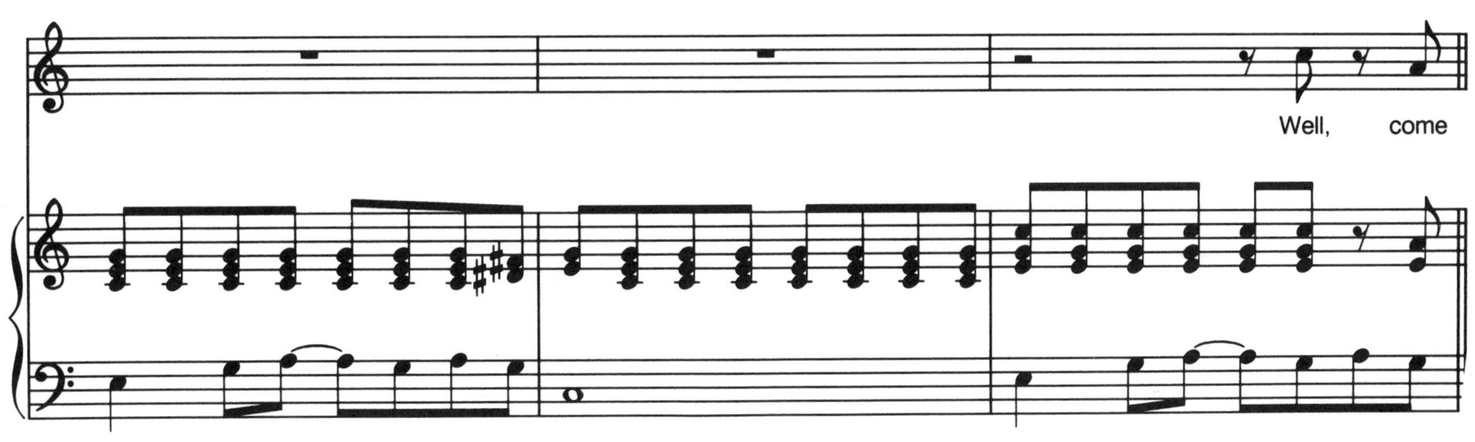
Well, come

C
on, pret - ty ba - by, won't you walk with me? Come
used to walk you home, ba - by, af - ter school,
on, pret - ty ba - by, won't you talk with me? Come
Car - ry your books home, too. But
on, pret - ty ba - by, give me one more chance.
now you got a boy - friend down the street,
Try and save our ro - mance! Slow down!
Ba - by what you tryin' a do? You bet - er slow down!

F
Ba - by, now you're mov - in' way too fast.
C
You got - ta

G
F
gim - me lit - tle lov - in',
gim - me lit - tle lov - in',
C
Ow!
Brrr!
Ow!
if you want our love to last.
To Coda
1
(2) Ow!
Well, I
2 C

F
C

G
F
3
C
C
Well, you know that I love you, tell the

would I do; Come on, pret - ty ba - by, why can't
you be true? I need your bod - y, ba - by,
D.S. al Coda
oh so bad, The best lit - tle wom - an I ev - er had, Slow down,
CODA
C
C9

SOMETHING

Words and Music by
GEORGE HARRISON

Am/G
D7
To Coda
F
Eb
G7/D
know I be-lieve_ and how.___
A
C#m/G#
F#m
F#m/E
You're ask-ing me_ will my_ love grow, I don't know_
D
G
You stick a - round_ now, it may
_____ I___ don't know.
C
show, I don't know_____ I___ don't know.

Cmaj7
C7
F
C/E
D7
G
Am7
G/B
Am
Am(♯7)
Am7
D9
D.S. al Coda
F
E♭
G7/D
CODA
F
E♭
G7/D
A
F
E♭
G7/D
C

STRAWBERRY FIELDS FOREVER

Words and Music by
JOHN LENNON and PAUL McCARTNEY

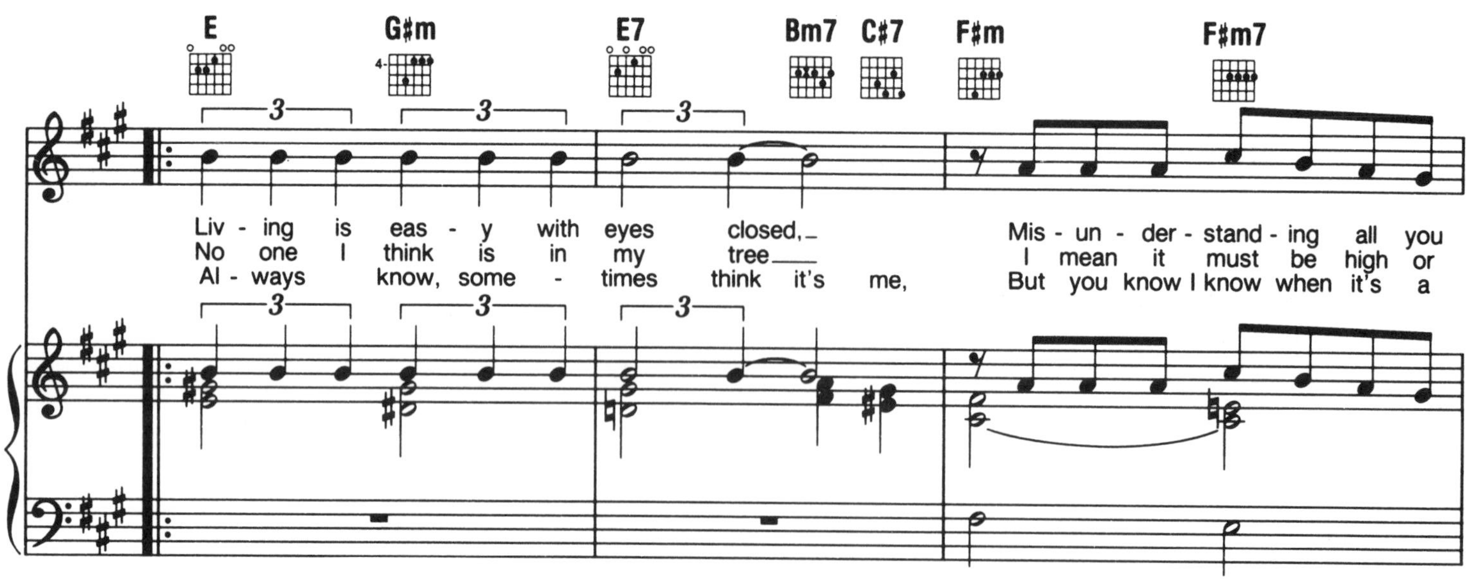
E
G#m
E7
Bm7
C#7
F#m
F#m7
Liv - ing is eas - y with eyes closed,
No one I think is in my tree
Al - ways know, some - times think it's me,
Mis - un - der - stand - ing all you
I mean it must be high or
But you know I know when it's a

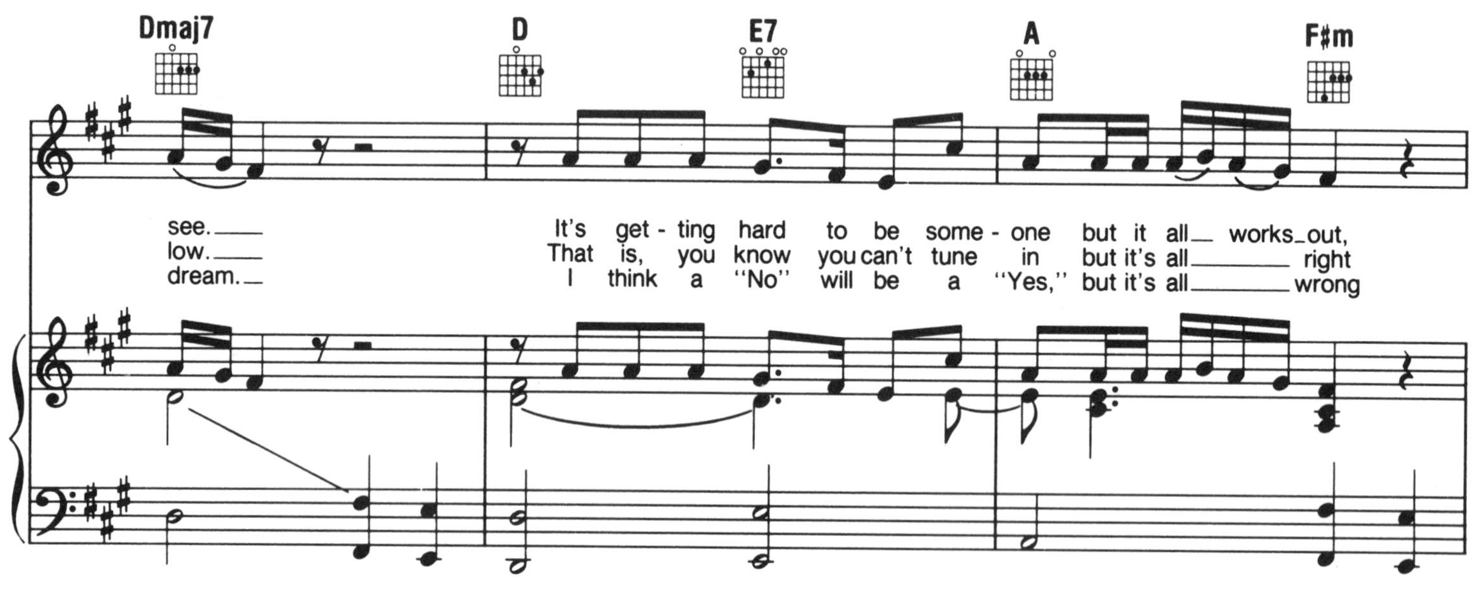
Dmaj7
D
E7
A
F#m
see.
low.
dream.
It's get - ting hard to be some - one but it all works out,
That is, you know you can't tune in but it's all right
I think a "No" will be a "Yes," but it's all wrong

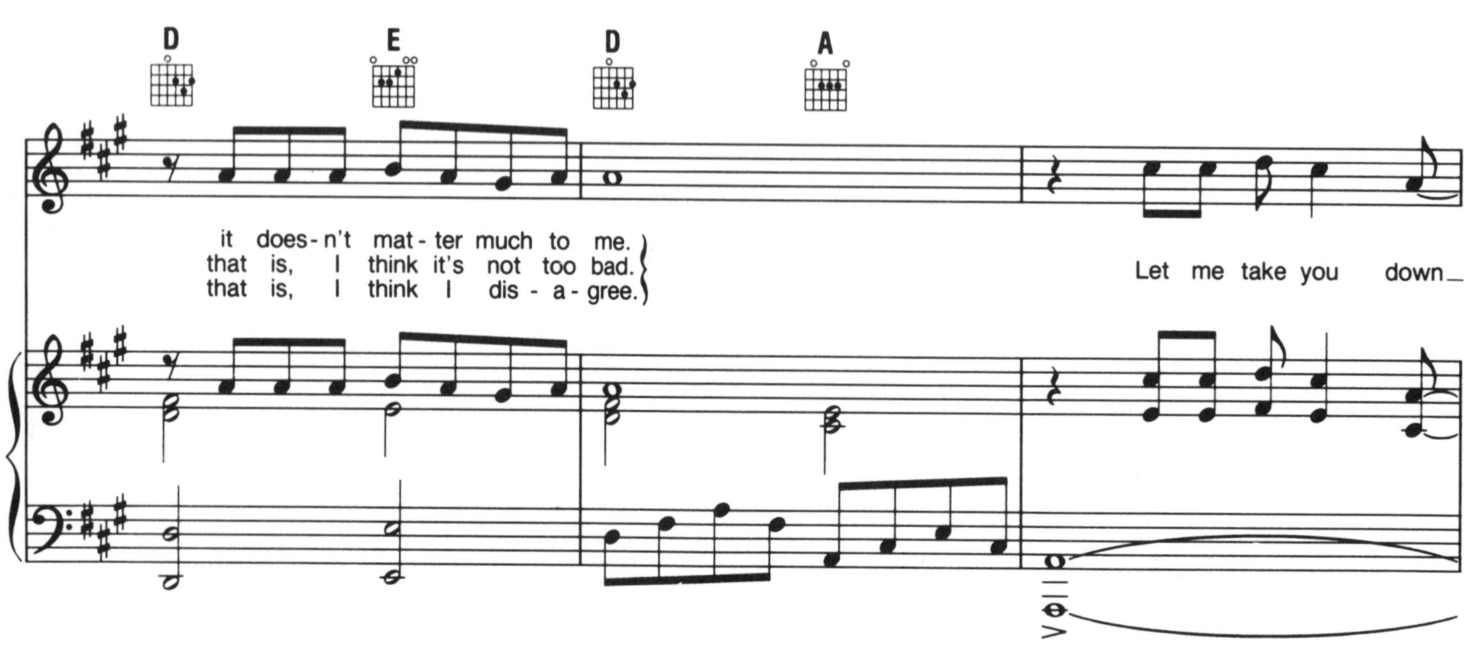
D
E
D
A
it does - n't mat - ter much to me.
that is, I think it's not too bad.
that is, I think I dis - a - gree.
Let me take you down

Em7
C♯dim
'cause I'm go-ing to Straw-ber-ry Fields. Noth-ing is
D
E
F♯
1,2
Dmaj7
A
real, and noth-ing to get hung a-bout... Straw-ber-ry Fields for-ev-er.
3
Dmaj7
A
F♯m
Dmaj7
Straw-ber-ry Fields for-ev-er, Straw-ber-ry Fields for-
A
Dmaj7
E
D
A
ev-er, Straw-ber-ry Fields for-ev-er.

SUN KING

Words and Music by
JOHN LENNON and PAUL McCARTNEY

F♯m
Gm
G♯m
E6
A
E6
G11
Ah
C
Cmaj9
C
Here
comes
the
G7
A7
Sun
King

F
D7
F
Ev - 'ry - bod - y's laugh - ing
Ev - 'ry - bod - y's hap -
D7
C
- py.
Here
Em7
C
C7
F
C
comes
the
Sun
F
G
A6
King.
Quan - do para mu - cho mi a -

B7
E6
mor - e de fe - li - ce cor - a - zon.
F♯m7
B7
mun - do pa - pa - raz - zi mi a - mor - e chick - a fer - dy pa - ra
E6
F♯m7
sol.
Cues - to ob - ri - ga - do tan - ta
B7
E6
mu - cho que can eat it car - ou - sel.

A TASTE OF HONEY

Words and Music by RIC MARLOW
and BOBBY SCOTT

B
F♯m
F♯m♯7
F♯m7
then, I feel up - on my lips a -
heart. There lin - gers still, though we're far a -
B
F♯m
gain, A taste of hon - ey (A taste of hon - ey)
part, That taste of hon - ey. (A taste of hon - ey)
A
E
F♯m
Bm
F♯m
Tast - ing much sweet - er than wine.
Bm
F♯m
Shuffle tempo
B
I will re - turn, Yes, I
3
3

F♯m
B
To Coda
A
E
will re - turn; I'll come back for the hon - ey and
F♯m
D.S. al Coda
you. (Doo dood - n' doo.) (Doo dood - n' doo.) Yours
CODA
Slower
A
E
back (He'll come back) for hon-ey (For the hon-ey) and
A tempo
F♯m
Bm
F♯m
Bm
F♯m
Bm
F♯
you.

TAXMAN

Words and Music by
GEORGE HARRISON
Moderate Rock
D7
Let me tell you how it will be:
per - cent ap - pear too small,
me what I want it for,
ad - vice for those who die,
D7(♯9)
D7
(Ah - ah, Mister Wil - son)
(Tax - man)
There's one for you, nine - teen for me.
Be thank - ful I don't take it all.
If you don't want to pay some more.
De - clare the pen - nies on your eyes.
D7(♯9)
D7
(Ah - ah, Mister
(Tax man)

C7
Heath.)
'Cause I'm the tax - man,
Yeah, I'm the

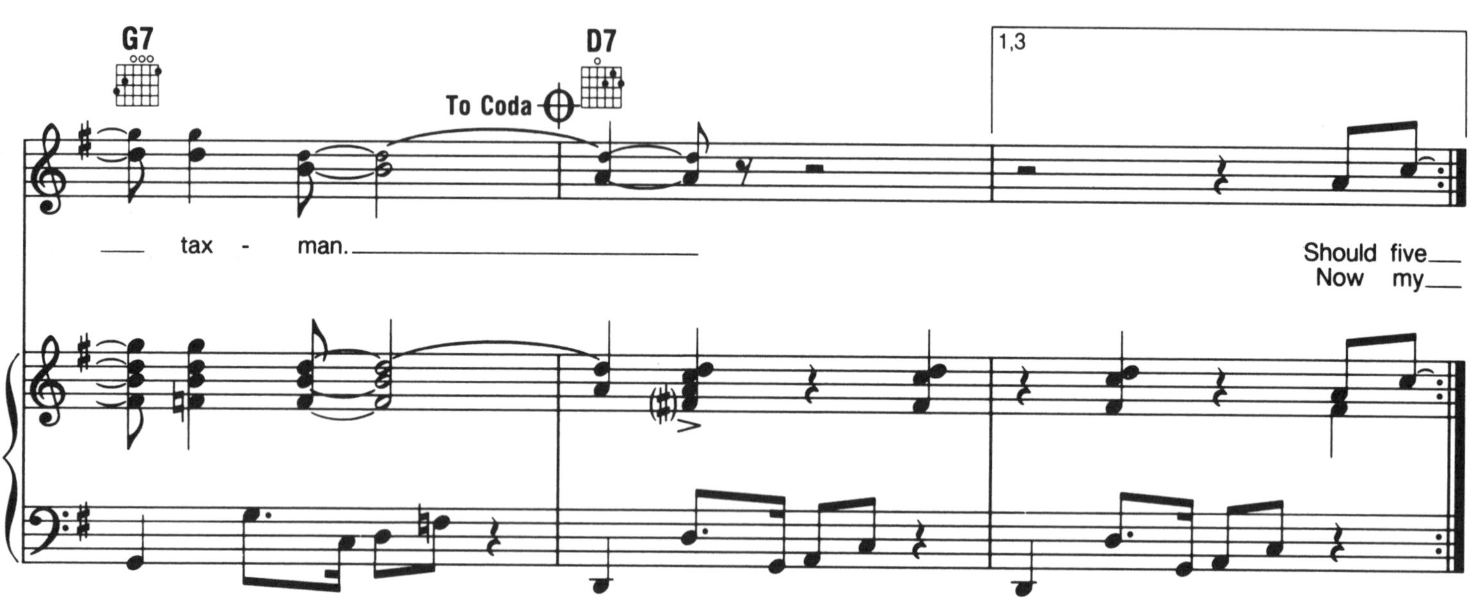
G7
D7
To Coda
1,3
tax - man.
Should five
Now my

2
D7
If you drive a car, car;
I'll tax

If you try to sit, sit;
the street;
I'll tax

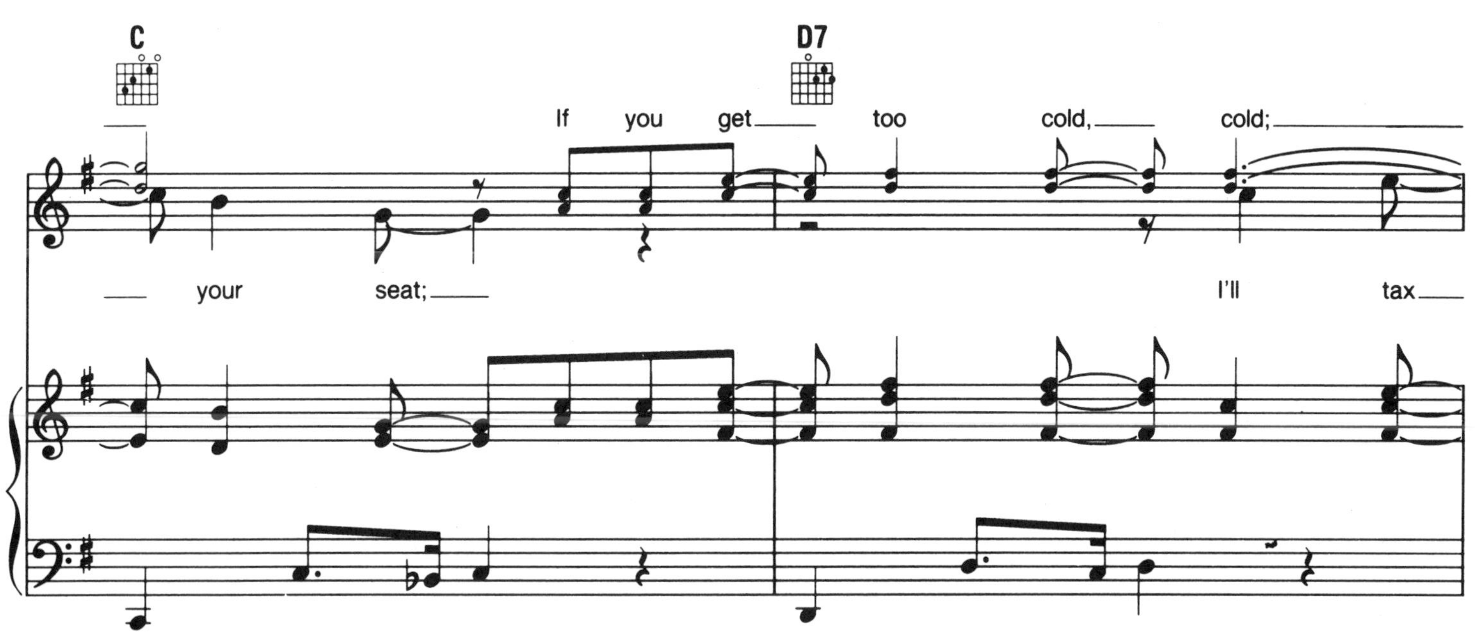
C
D7
If you get too cold, cold;
your seat;
I'll tax

C
If you take a walk, walk.
the heat;
I'll tax your feet.

D7
Tax - man!
'Cause I'm the
C7
G7
tax - man,
Yeah,
I'm the
tax - man.

D7
D.S. al Coda
(with repeats)
CODA
D7
Don't ask
And you're
F7
E7
D7
work - ing for no one but me.

TELL ME WHAT YOU SEE

Words and Music by
JOHN LENNON and PAUL McCARTNEY

G
C
G
O - pen up your eyes now,
Look in - to these eyes now,
O - pen up your eyes now,
C
G
C
Tell me what you see
Tell me what you see
Tell me what you see
It is no sur - prise
Don't you re - al - ize
It is no sur - prise
G
C
D
1
G
now
now
now
What you see is me.

2,3,4
G
Dm/G
1,2 Tell me what you
3 Mm mm mm mm
C
see.
mm.
To Coda
G
D7
G
1
2
D.S. al Coda
CODA
G

THANK YOU GIRL

Words and Music by
JOHN LENNON and PAUL McCARTNEY

D
A
D
G
be in love with you.
fool would doubt our love.
And all I got - ta
A
G
A
To Coda
do is thank you, girl,
thank you, girl.
Bm
D
A7
Thank you, girl, for lov - in' me the way that you do.
Em
A
D
(Way that you do)
That's the kind of love that is too good to be true.

G
A
G
And all I got - ta do is thank you, girl,
A
D.C. al Coda
thank you, girl,
CODA
A
G
A
G
D
G
D
G
Ow!
Ow!
Ow!
A
G
D
G/D
D
G/D
D
Ow!
Ow!

TELL ME WHY

Words and Music by
JOHN LENNON and PAUL McCARTNEY

Em7
A7
D6
and why you lied to me.
Em7
A7
D
Bm7
1. Well, I gave you ev - 'ry - thing I had, But you
2. If it's some - thing that I've said or done, Tell me
Em7
A7
D
left me sit - ing on my own. Did you have to treat me oh so bad?
what, and I'll a - pol - o - gize. If you don't I real - ly can't go on.
Bm7
Em7
1
A7
A13
All I do is hang my head and moan. Tell me
Hold - ing back these tears in my eyes.

2
A7
A13
D
Bm7
Em7
Tell me why you cried, and why you
A7
D
Em7
A7
D
lied to me. Tell me why
Bm7
Em7
To Coda
A7
D6
you cried, and why you lied to me.
D7
G7
Well, I beg you on my bend - ed knees, If you'll

A7
Bm
on - ly lis - ten to my pleas. Is there an - y - thing I can
Em
A7
do 'Cause I real - ly can't stand it, I'm so in love with
D.S. al Coda
D
A13
CODA
A7
you. Tell me
lied to
Bm7
B♭7
A7sus
A13
D
me.

THERE'S A PLACE

Words and Music by
JOHN LENNON and PAUL McCARTNEY

B♭
Fmaj7
B♭
Gm
3
and there's no time when I'm a-
Dm
To Coda
no chord
F
lone. I think of you
B♭
F
B♭
F
and things you do go round my head,
Dm
C
B♭
the things you've said, like "I love

C
Dm
on - ly you." ___
In my mind there's no
G
F
A
Dm
sor - row. ___
Don't you know that it's so?
There'll be no sad to -
G
F
A
Dm
no chord
mor - row. ___
Don't you know that it's so?
There ___
D.S. al Coda
___ is a
CODA
no chord
F
B♭
Repeat and Fade
There's a place.
There's a

THINK FOR YOURSELF

Words and Music by
GEORGE HARRISON

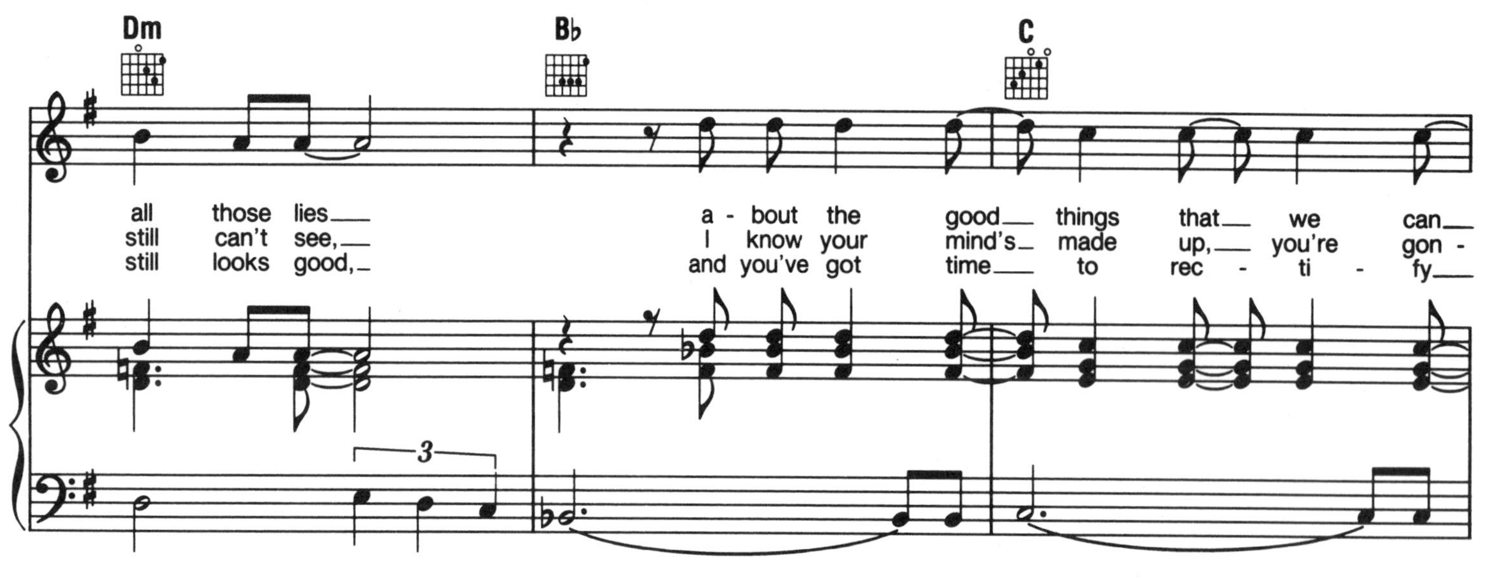
Dm
B♭
C
all those lies a - bout the good things that we can
still can't see, I know your mind's made up, you're gon -
still looks good, and you've got time to rec - ti - fy

G
Am
C7
have if we close our eyes.
na cause more mis - er - y.
all the things that you should.
Do what you want to do,

G7
and go where you're go - ing to,

E♭
D7
To Coda
1,2
G
Think for your - self, 'cause I won't be there with you.
3
G
D.S. al Coda
you.
CODA
C7
G
E♭
you.
Think for your - self 'cause
D7
C7
G
I won't be there with you.

THINGS WE SAID TODAY

Am
C
C9
Some- day when I'm lone - ly
Some- day when we're dream - ing
F
B♭
Am
Em7
wish- ing you weren't so far a - way,
deep in love, not a lot to say,
Then I will re - mem -
Then we will re - mem -
Am
Em7
Am
Em7
1 Am
- ber things we said to - day.
- ber things we said to - day.
2 A
D7
Me, I'm just the luck - y kind,

B7
E7
A
Love to hear you say that love is love. And though we may
D7
B7
B♭
be blind, Love is here to stay and that's e - nough
Am
Em7
Am
Em7
Am
Em7
to make you mine girl, be the on - ly one.
Am
Em7
Am
Em7
Am
Em7
Love me all the time, girl,

Am
Em7
Am
C
we'll go on and on.
Some- day when we're
C9
F
B♭
dream - ing,
deep in love not a lot so say,
Am
Em7
Am
Em7
1 Am
Em7
A
Then we will re - mem - ber
things we said to - day.
2 Am
Em7
Am
Repeat and Fade
things we said to - day.

THIS BOY
(RINGO'S THEME)

Words and Music by
JOHN LENNON and PAUL McCARTNEY

1
Dmaj7
Bm
Em
A7
gain.
2
Dmaj7
D
D7
gain.
Oh, and
G
F♯7
this boy would be hap - py just to
Bm
D7
love you. But oh, my! Oh,

G
E7
that boy won't be hap py
A7
A7sus
A7
F♯m/A
A
till he's seen you cry.
Dmaj7
Bm
Em
A7
This boy would - n't mind the
Dmaj7
Bm
Em
A7
pain, Would al - ways feel the

Dmaj7
Bm
Em7
A7
same
If this boy gets you back a -
Dmaj7
Bm
Em
A7
gain.
Dmaj7
Bm
Em
A7
This boy,
Dmaj7
Bm
Em
A7
Repeat and Fade
This boy,

TICKET TO RIDE

Words and Music by
JOHN LENNON and PAUL McCARTNEY

D7
F♯m
G
She's got a tick - et to ri - hi - hide,
F♯m
E7
A
She's got a tick - et to ride, but she don't care!
She
A
D7
I don't know why she's rid - in' so high,
she ought - ta think twice; she ought - ta do right by me.
E
Be -

D7
fore she gets to say-in' good-bye
she ought-ta think twice, she ought-ta do right by
E
A
me.
1. I think I'm gon-na be sad,
2. She said that liv-ing with me
I think it's to-day
is bring-in' her down
yeah!
yeah!
The
For
Bm7
girl that's driv-ing me mad
she would nev-er be free
is go-ing a-way.
when I was a-round.
Yeah!

E7
F♯m
D7
Oh, she's got a tick - et to ride,
F♯m
G
F♯m
She's got a tick - et to ri - hi - hide,
She's got a tick - et to ride,
E7
1 A
but she don't care!
I
2 A
Repeat and Fade
My ba - by don't care!

TILL THERE WAS YOU

(From "THE MUSIC MAN")

Words and Music by
MEREDITH WILLSON

Gm7 Gm7/C C7 | 1 F Gm7 C7

all till there was you.
all till There were

2 F F7 B♭

there was you. Then there was mu - sic

B♭m F D7

and won - der - ful ros - es, they tell me, in

Gm7 G7 C7

sweet, fra - grant mea - dows of dawn and

C+
F
F♯dim7
dew. There was love all a - round but I
Gm7
B♭m
F
F/A
A♭m6
nev - er heard it sing - ing, No, I nev - er heard it at
Gm7
Gm7/C
C7
F
To Coda
Gm7
C7
all, till there was you.
F
F♯dim7
Gm7

B♭m
F
Am7
A♭m7
Gm7
G♭7♯9
F
Cdim7
F7
D.S. al Coda
CODA
F
Then there was
C7
C+
C7
F
Till
there was you.
D♭7
F
Fmaj7

TOMORROW NEVER KNOWS

Words and Music by
JOHN LENNON and PAUL McCARTNEY

Lay down all thoughts, surren-
That ig-nor-ance and hate
-der to the void; It is
may mourn the dead, It is be-
Bb/C
C
shin-ing, it is shin-ing
liev-ing, it is be-liev-ing.
That you may see the mean-ing of with-in,
But lis-ten to the col-or of your dream,

Bb/C
It is be - ing,
It is not liv - ing,
C
To Coda
it is be - ing.
it is not liv - ing.

3
3

Bb/C
C
D.S. al Coda
That love
CODA
C
Or play the game "Ex - is - tence" to the end
Bb/C
of the be - gin - ning,
C
Repeat and Fade
of the be - gin - ning,
of the be -

WE CAN WORK IT OUT

Words and Music by
JOHN LENNON and PAUL McCARTNEY

Bm
Bm/A
Bm/G
Life is ver - y short and there's no time
F♯sus
F♯
Bm
Bm/A
for fuss - ing and fight - ing, my friend.
Bm/G
Bm/F♯
Bm
Bm/A
I have al - ways thought that it's a crime
Bm/G
F♯sus
F♯
Bm
Bm/A
so I will ask you once a -

Bm/G
Bm/F♯
D
Dsus
D
gain.
Try to see it my way,
Dsus
C(add9)
D
Dsus
D
on-ly time will tell if I am right or I am wrong.
While you see it your way
Dsus
C(add9)
D
G
D
there's a chance that we might fall a - part be-fore too long.
We can work it out,
G
Asus
A
D
G6/D
D
we can work it out.

TWIST AND SHOUT

Words and Music by
BURT RUSSELL and PHIL MEDLEY

D
G
A7
D
G
ba - by now,
Come on and work it on out.
(Come on ba - by)
(Work it on out)
A7
D
G
1. Well, work it on out,
2,3. You know you twist, lit - tle girl,
(Work it on out)
(Twist lit - tle girl)
A7
D
G
A7
You know you look so good.
You know you twist so fine.
(Look so good)
(Twist so fine)
You know you got me
Come on and twist a lit - tle
D
G
A7
go - in' now,
clos - er now,
(Got me goin')
(Twist a lit - tle clos - er)
Just like I knew you would.
And let me know that you're

D
G
To Coda
1 A7
2 A7
(Like I knew you would)
Well, shake it up ba
mine. (Let me know you're mine)
D
G
A
G
A
D
G
A
G
A
D
G
A
G
A
D
G
A
G
A
Ah
Ah

A7
D.S. al Coda
Ah
Ah
Ah
Shake it up ba -
CODA
A7
D
G
Well, shake it, shake it, shake it, ba - by, now,
(Shake it up ba -
A7
D
G
A
Well, shake it, shake it, shake it, ba - by now.
- by.)
(Shake it up, ba - by.)
Ah
A7
D
Dmaj9
Ah
Ah
Ah

TWO OF US

Words and Music by
JOHN LENNON and PAUL McCARTNEY

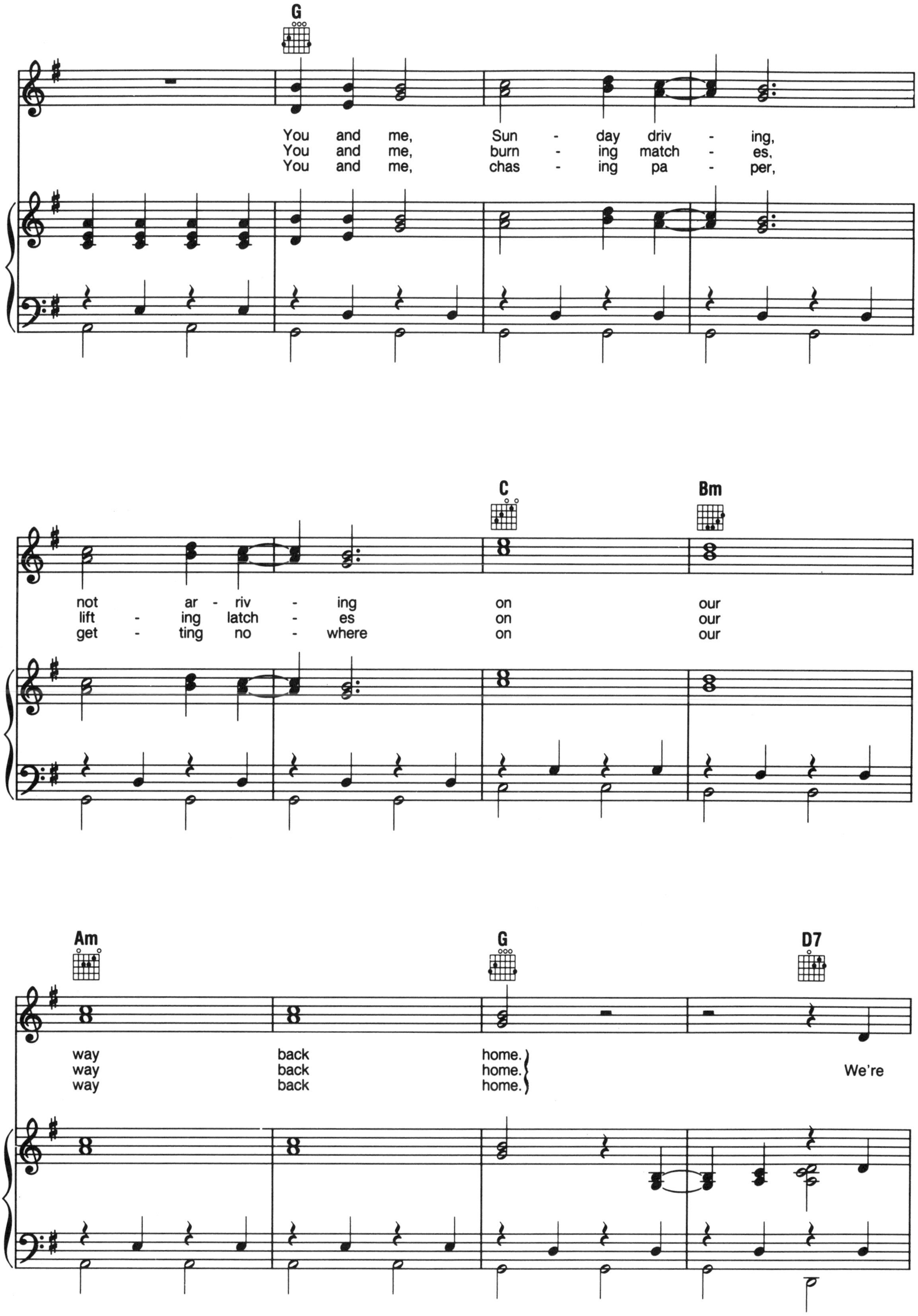

G

You and me, Sun - day driv - ing,
You and me, burn - ing match - es,
You and me, chas - ing pa - per,

C Bm

not ar - riv - ing on our
lift - ing latch - es on our
get - ting no - where on our

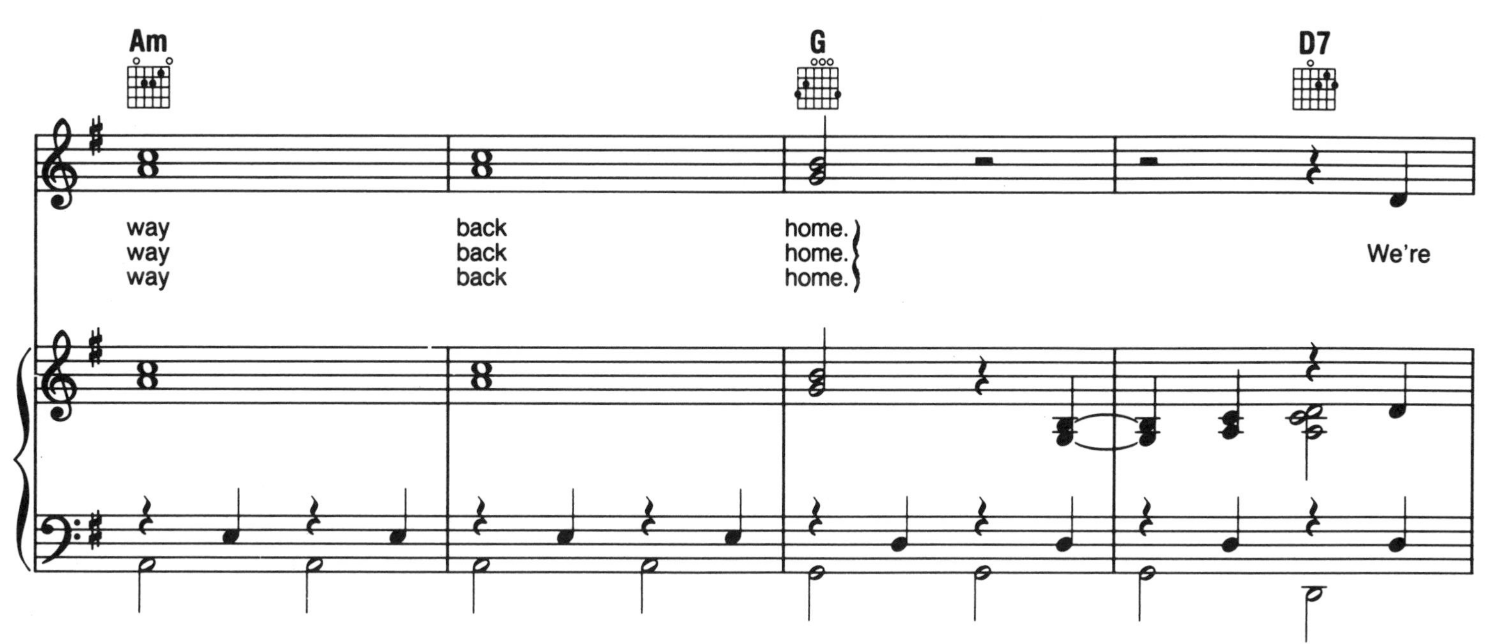

G
D7
on our way home, We're on our way
G
D7
G
To Coda
1
home. We're go - in' home.
2,3
B♭
You and I
Dm
Gm
have mem - o - ries long - er than

Am
the road that stretch - es out a - head.
D11
D7
D.S.
D.S. al Coda
CODA
G
G
Repeat and Fade
(Spoken:) We're go-in' home.
Better believe it.
Goodbye.

WAIT

Words and Music by
JOHN LENNON and PAUL McCARTNEY

A
Dmaj7
A
Dmaj7
A
Dmaj7
Wait till I come back to your side, we'll for -
A
C#7
F#m
F#m
get the tears we cried. But if your I feel as
Bm
E
A
though you ought to know that I've been good, as good as I can
F#m
Bm
E
be. And if you do, I'll trust in you and know that

A
F♯m
C♯
F♯m7
B/F♯
you will wait for me.
It's been a long time,
But if your heart breaks,
Bm/F♯
F♯m
C♯7
F♯m
now I'm coming back home, I've been a-
don't wait, turn me a-way. And if your
F♯m7
B/F♯
Bm/F♯
F♯m
way now, oh, how
heart's strong, hold on,
C♯7
F♯m
A
Dmaj7
I've been a-lone.
I won't de-lay.
Wait till I

A
Dmaj7
A
Dmaj7
A
C♯7
come back to your side
we'll for - get the tears we cried.
F♯m
I feel as
F♯m
It's been a long time,
F♯m7
B/F♯
Bm/F♯
F♯m
C♯7
F♯m
now I'm com - ing back home, I've been a - way now,
F♯m7
B/F♯
Bm/F♯
C♯7
F♯m
oh how I've been a - lone.
rit.

WHAT GOES ON

Words and Music by JOHN LENNON
PAUL McCARTNEY and RICHARD STARKEY

E
You are tear - ing me a - part
when you treat
me so un - kind.
A7
What goes on
Bsus
B7
in your mind?
To Coda
E

E
The oth - er day I saw you as I
I met you in the morn - ing wait - ing
used to think of no one else but

Am
E
walked a - long the road. But when I saw you with
for the tides of time. But now the tides are turn -
you were just the same. You did - n't e - ven think

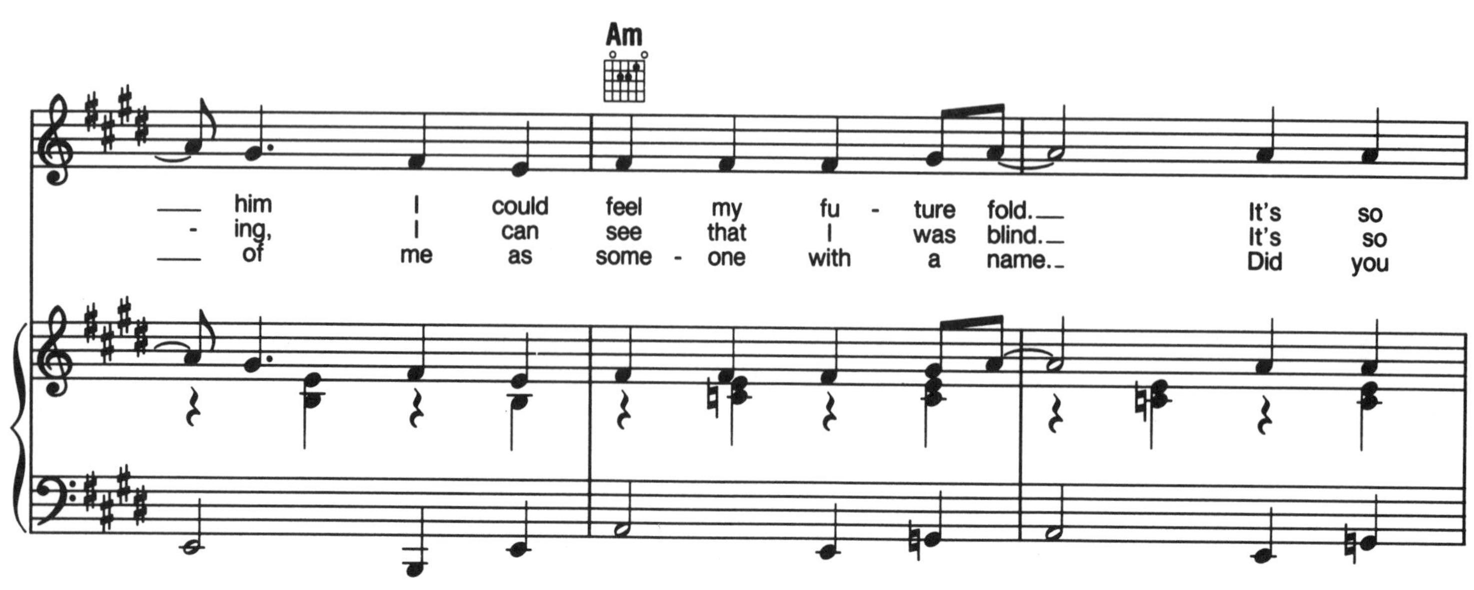
Am
him I could feel my fu - ture fold. It's so
- ing, I can see that I was blind. It's so
of me as some - one with a name. Did you

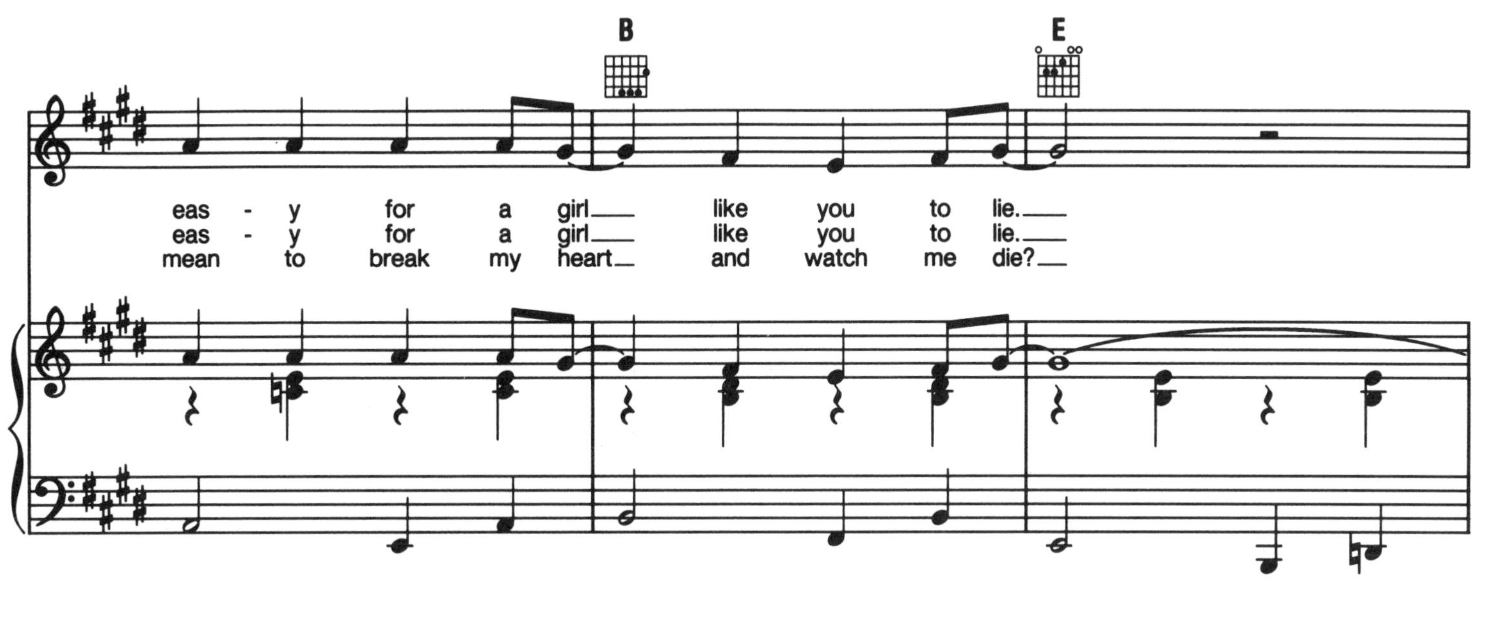
B
E
eas - y for a girl like you to lie.
eas - y for a girl like you to lie.
mean to break my heart and watch me die?

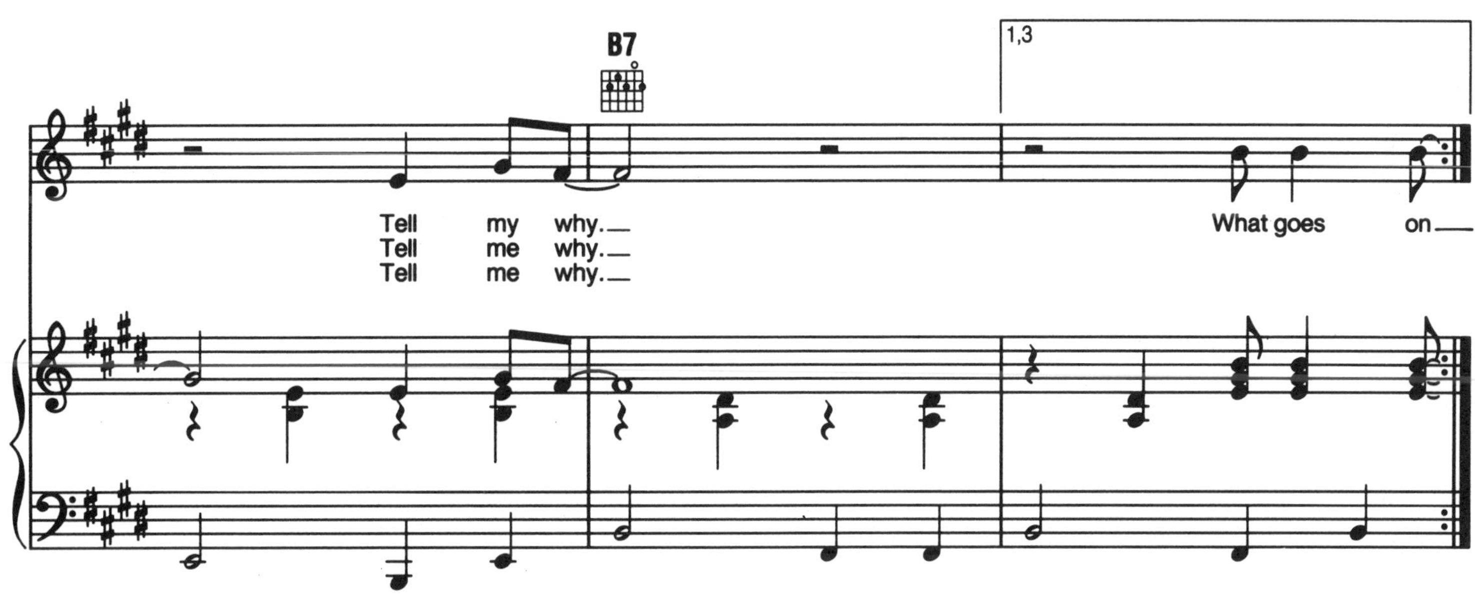
B7
1,3
Tell my why.
Tell me why.
Tell me why.
What goes on

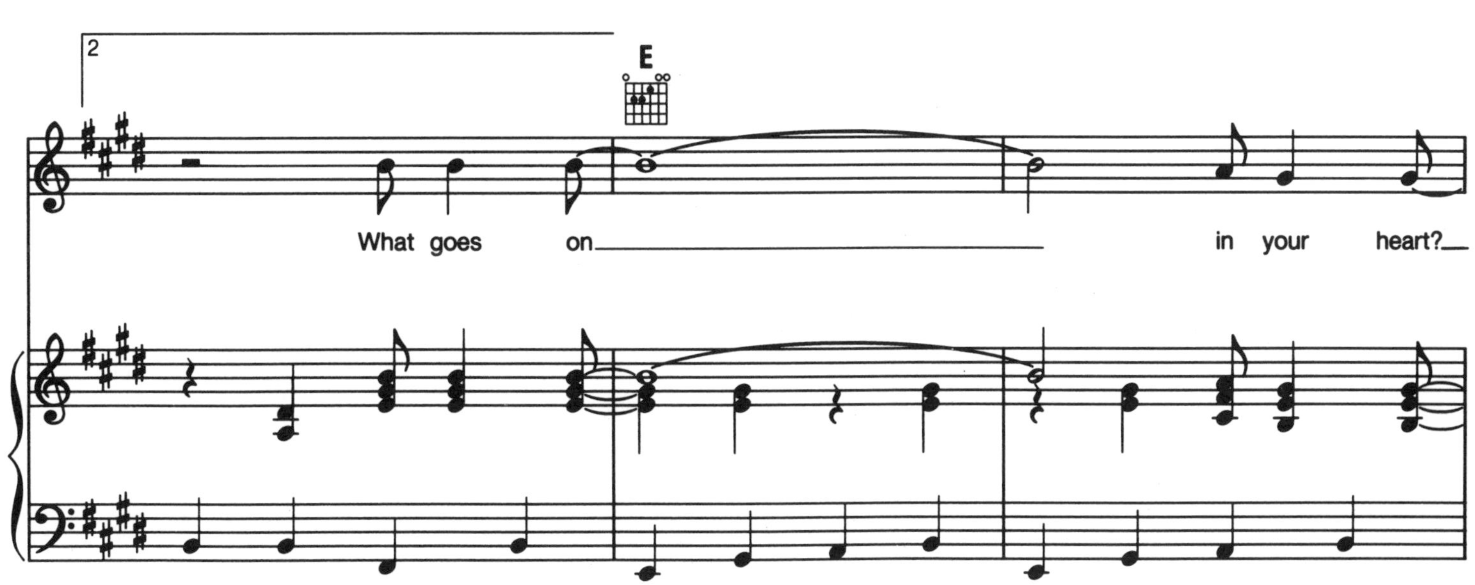
2
E
What goes on in your heart?

A
E

A7
B7
E7
D.S. al Coda
CODA
E
E7
E
3

WHAT YOU'RE DOING

Words and Music by JOHN LENNON
and PAUL McCARTNEY

D
G
do - in'
to
me?
do - in'
to
D
G
Bm
me?
I've been wait - ing
here for you
G7
Bm
won - d'rin' what
you're gon - na
do.
Em
And should you need
a love that's true,
it's

A
D
me.
Please stop you're
G
D
G
ly - in'.
You got me cry - in', girl.
Why should it
Bm
G
To Coda
be so much to ask of you what you're do - in' to
D
G
D
me?

G7
D
G7
Bm
G7
D
G
D.S. al Coda
I've been wait - ing
CODA
D
G
me,
what you're do - in'
to

D
G
D
me,
what you're do - in'
to
me?
G
D
A
D
G
D
G
Repeat and Fade

WHILE MY GUITAR GENTLY WEEPS

Words and Music by
George Harrison

D
E7
Am
I look at the floor
Am/G
F♯m7-5
Fmaj7
and I see it needs sweep - ing;
Am
G
C
Still my gui - tar gen - tly weeps.
E7
A
C♯m
I don't know why
I don't know why

F♯m
C♯m
Bm
no - bod - y told you
you were di - vert - ed,
how to un -
you were per -
E7
D/F♯
E7
fold your love.
vert - ed, too.
A
C♯m
F♯m
I don't know how
I don't know how
some - one con -
you were in -
C♯m
Bm
trolled you,
vert - ed,
they bought and sold you.
no one a - lert - ed you.

E7
D/F#
Am
I look at the world
I look at you all,
Am/G
F#m7-5
Fmaj7
and I notice its turning
see the love there that's sleeping
Am
G
D
While my guitar gently weeps.
While my guitar gently weeps.
E
To Coda
Am
Am/G
For ev'ry mistake we must sure-
Look

F#m7-5
Fmaj7
Am
-ly___ be learn - ing;
Still my gui - tar___
G
C
E
___ gen - tly weeps._
Am
Am/G
F#m7-5
Fmaj7
Am
Am/G

D
E
Am
Am/G
F♯m7-5
Fmaj7
Am
G
C
E
D.S. al Coda
CODA
Am
Am/G
at you all.

F#m7-5
Fmaj7
Am
Still my gui - tar
G
C
E7
gen - tly weeps.
Am
Am/G
F#m7-5
Fmaj7
Am
Am/G
D
E7
Repeat and Fade

WHEN I GET HOME

Words and Music by JOHN LENNON
and PAUL McCARTNEY

C7 F7 C7

on, on my way, 'cause I'm a - gon - na see my ba - by to -
on, if you please, I got no time for triv - i - al - i -
on, let me through, I got so man - y things I got - ta

F7 C7 F7

day; I've got a whole lot - ta things I got - ta say to
ties; I've got a girl who's wait - ing home for me to -
do; I've got no bus - 'ness be - in' here with you this

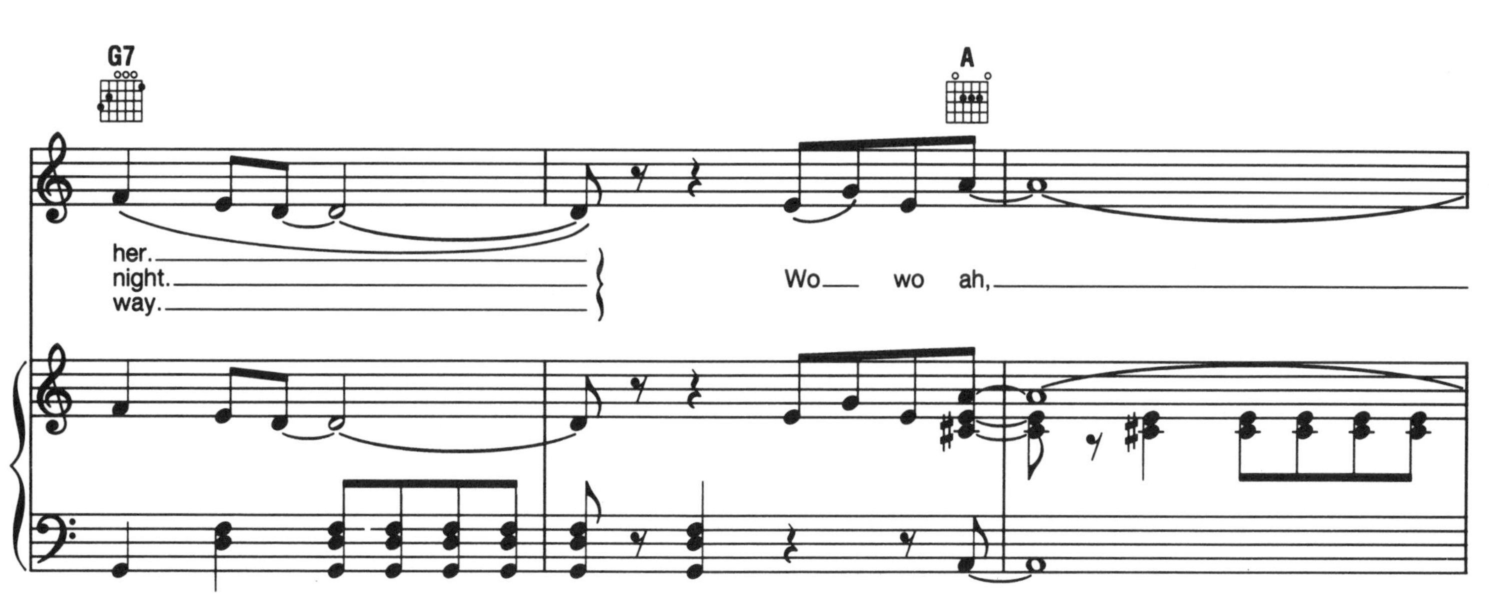

A
wo wo ah,
I got a
To Coda
D9
G7
no chord
1
Am
G7
whole lot - ta things to tell her when I get home.
2
Am
Come
When I'm get - ting
C
Am
C7
home to - night, I'm gon - na hold her tight, I'm gon - na love her till the cows come home.

Am
F
G7
F
I bet I'll love her more till I walk out that door
G7
Am
G7
D.S. al Coda
a - gain.
Come
CODA
G7
A
when I get home,
Yeah,
I got a
D9
G7
C
whole lot - ta things to tell her
when I get home.

WHEN I'M SIXTY FOUR

Words and Music by
JOHN LENNON and PAUL McCARTNEY

no chord
C
birth - day greet - ings bot - tle of wine?
If I'd been out till
C7
F
quar - ter to three
would you lock the door?
Ab7-5/Gb
C/G
A7
D9
G7/6
Will you still need me,
will you still feed me
when I'm six - ty
C
Am
four?
Oo

G
Am
You'll be old - er,
E
Am
too.
Ah,
Dm
and if you say the word
F
G
C
I could stay with you.

G
C
I could be hand - y
Send me a post - card,
mend - ing a fuse
drop me a line
when your lights have gone.
stat - ing point of view.
G7
You can knit a sweat - er by the fire - side,
In - di - cate pre - cise - ly what you mean to say
no chord
Sun - day morn - ing
Yours sin - cere - ly
C
go for a ride.
wast - ing a - way.
Do - ing the gar - den, dig - ging the weeds,
Give me your an - swer, fill in a form,

C7
F
Ab7-5/Gb
Who could ask for more?
Mine for - ev - er more.
Will you still need me,
Will you still need me,
C/G
A7
D9
G7/6
To Coda
C
will you still feed me,
will you still feed me,
When I'm six - ty four?
When I'm six - ty
Am
G
Ev - 'ry sum - mer we can rent a cot - tage in the Isle of Wight if it's not too dear.
Am
E
We shall scrimp and save;

Am
Dm
Grand - chil - dren on your knee;
F
G
C
Ve - ra, Chuck and Dave.
G
D.S. al Coda
CODA
C
four? Ho!
F
G7
C

WHY DON'T WE DO IT IN THE ROAD

Words and Music by
JOHN LENNON and PAUL McCARTNEY

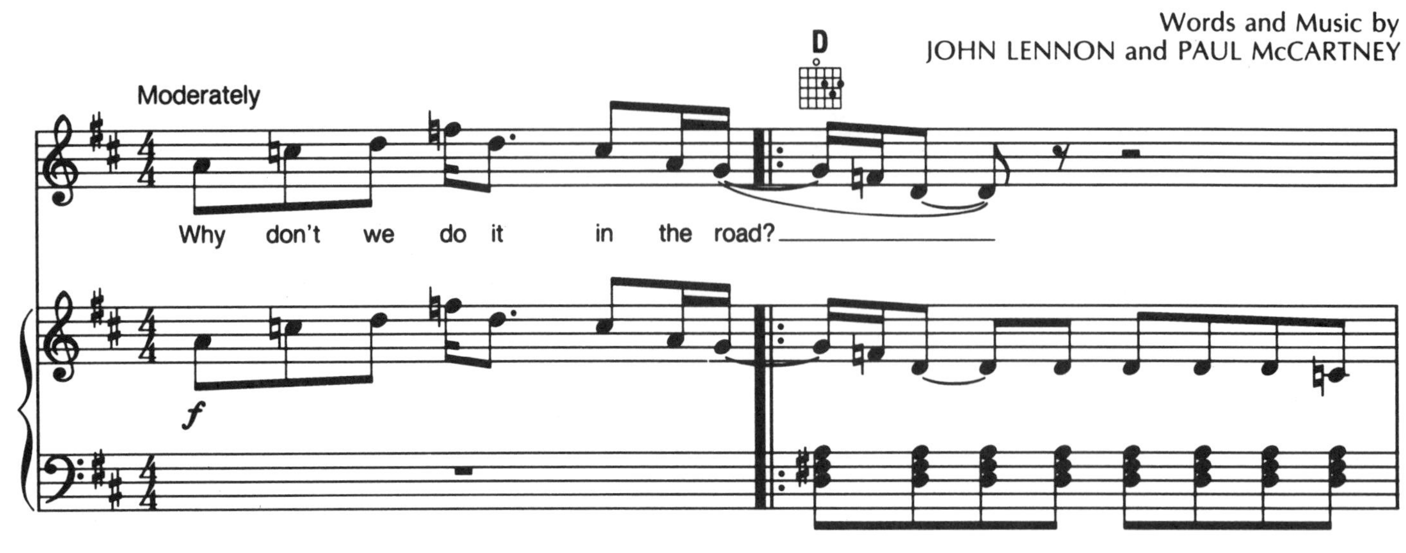

Why don't we do it in the road?

D7 G G7

Why don't we do it in the road? Why don't we do it in the road?

D7
A7
No one will be watch - ing us; Why
1
G7
D7
don't we do it in the road?
Why don't we do it in the road?
2
G7
D7
don't we do it in the road?
Oh,
D
Why don't we do it in the road?

Why don't we do it in the road?
D7
G7
Why dont' we do it, do it in the road?
D7
Why don't we do it in the road?
No
A7
G7
D7
one will be watch-ing us;
Why don't we do it in the road?

WILD HONEY PIE

Words and Music by JOHN LENNON
and PAUL McCARTNEY

WITH A LITTLE HELP FROM MY FRIENDS

Words and Music by JOHN LENNON
and PAUL McCARTNEY

F♯m
B7
you a song. and I'll try not to sing out of key.
of the day? (Are you sad be - cause you're on your own?)
out the light?) I can't tell you, but I know it's mine.
3

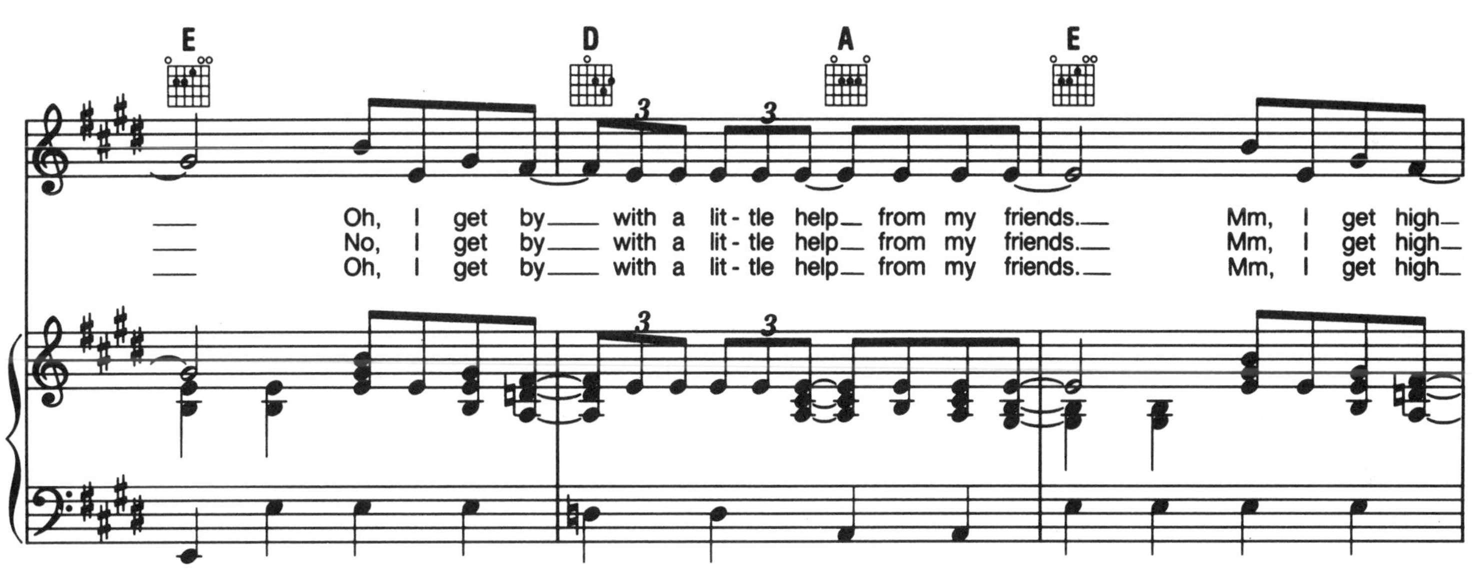
E
D
A
E
Oh, I get by with a lit - tle help from my friends. Mm, I get high
No, I get by with a lit - tle help from my friends. Mm, I get high
Oh, I get by with a lit - tle help from my friends. Mm, I get high
3

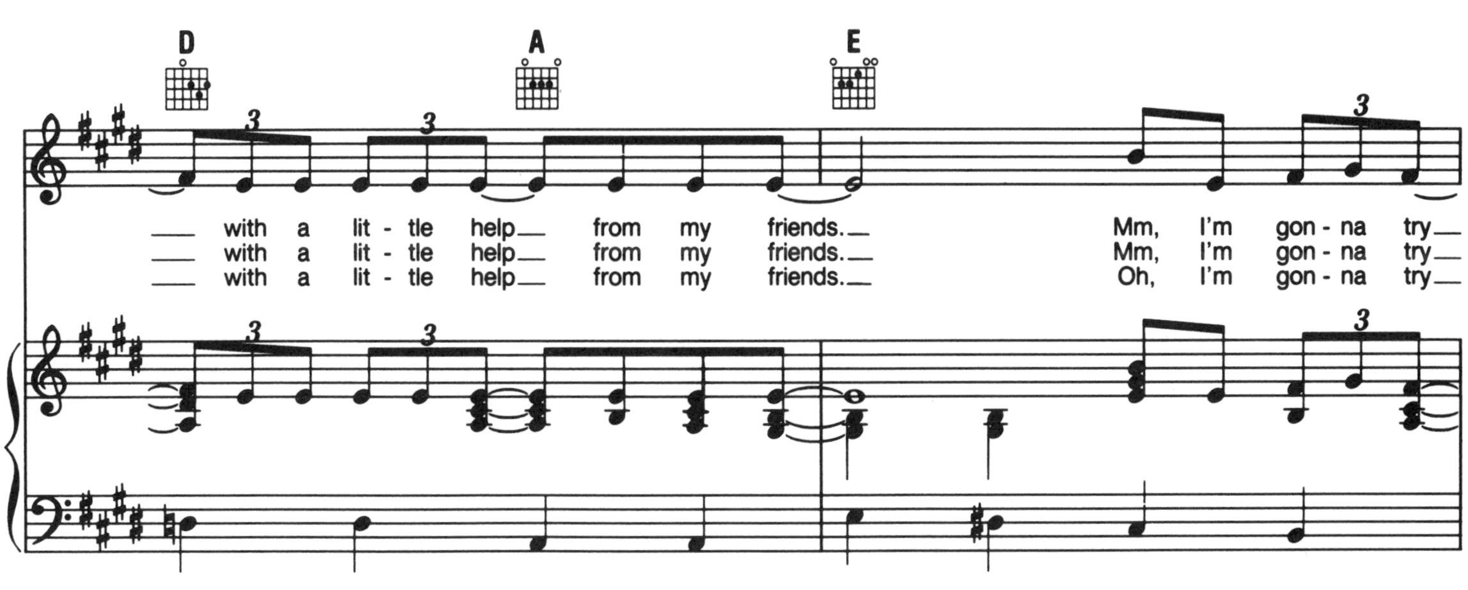
D
A
E
with a lit - tle help from my friends. Mm, I'm gon - na try
with a lit - tle help from my friends. Mm, I'm gon - na try
with a lit - tle help from my friends. Oh, I'm gon - na try
3

A
1
E
B7
with a lit - tle help from my friends.
with a lit - tle help from my friends.
with a lit - tle help from my friends.
2,3.
E
C♯m
F♯7
(Do you need an - y - bod - y?) I
(Do you need an - y - bod - y?) I
E
D
A
C♯m
need some - bod - y to love.
just need some - one to love.
(Could it be an - y - bod -
(Could it be an - y - bod -
F♯7
E
D
To Coda
A
D.S. al Coda
(3rd ending)
- y?) I want some - bod - y to love.
- y?) I want some - bod - y to love.

CODA
A
D
A
Oh, I get by with a lit-tle help from my friends.
E
D
A
E
Mm, I'm gon-na try with a lit-tle help from my friends. Oh, I get high
A
E
D
with a lit-tle help from my friends. Yes, I get by with a lit-tle help from my friends,
A
C/G
Am6
E
with a lit-tle help from my friends.

WITHIN YOU WITHOUT YOU

Words and Music by
GEORGE HARRISON

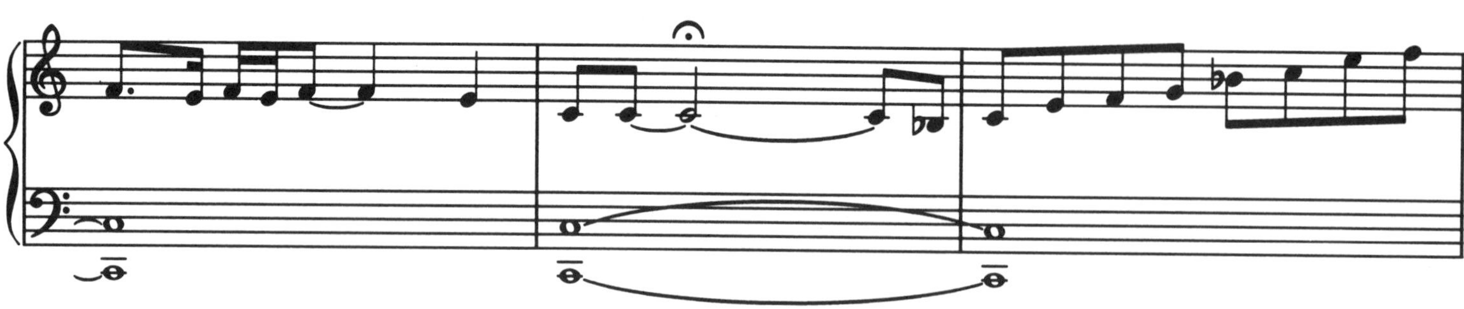

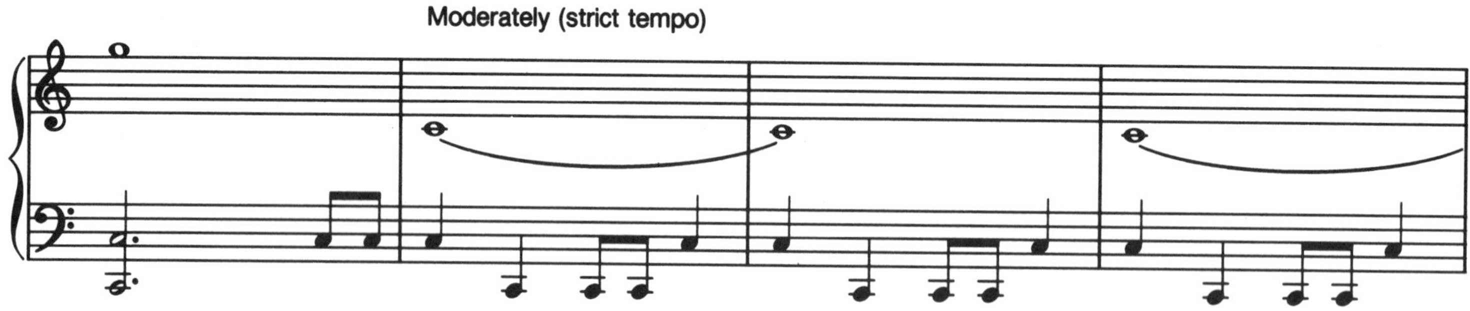

space be - tween us all, And the peo - ple
love we all could share, When we find it
who hide them - selves be - hind a
to try our best to hold it
1
wall of il - lu - sion,
there with our
nev - er glimpse the truth,
then it's far too late,
and they pass a -

way.
2
We were love, with our love we could save the world.
If they on - ly knew.
3
3
3
Slightly faster

Try to re - a - lize it's all with - in your - self, no
And to see you're real - ly on - ly ver - y small, and
1
one else can make you change.
2
life flows on with - in you and with - out you.
With movement

Freely

Moderately (strict tempo)
We were talk - ing a -
bout the love that's gone so cold, And the

peo - ple who gain the world and
lose their soul. They don't know, they can't
see. Are you one of them?
3
3

When you've seen be - yond your - self, then you may find peace
And the time will come when you see we're all one, and
1
of mind is wait - ing there.
2
life flows on with - in you and with - out you.

THE WORD

Moderately
G7
D7
Words and Music by
JOHN LENNON and PAUL McCARTNEY
mf
Say the
1,3.word and you'll be free. Say the word and be like
2.word and you'll be free. Spread the word and be like
4.word a chance to say that the word is just the
me. Say the word I'm think-ing of. Have you
me. Spread the word I'm think-ing of. Have you
way. It's the word I'm think-ing of. And you

D7
G/A
A
heard? The word is "love".
heard? The word is "love".
on - ly word is "love".
It's so fine, it's

F/G
G
D7
sun - shine. It's the word "love."

1,2,3
Dm
C
1. In the be - gin - ning I mis - un - der - stood,
2. Ev - 'ry - where I go I hear it said,
3. Now that I know what I feel must be right,

F
G
but now I've got it, the word is good. Spread the
in the good and the bad books that I have read. Say the
I'm here to show ev - 'ry - bod - y the light. Give the
4
Dm
C/D
Dm7
G/D
D7
Say the
word
"love".
Say the word,
G7

D7
"love".
Say the word,
"love".
Say the
Dm
A+
F/G
G9
D7
word,
"love".
Dm
C/D
Dm7
G/D
Dm

WORDS OF LOVE

Words and Music by
BUDDY HOLLY

D
E
A
D
E
Mmm.
Words of love you whis - per soft and
A
D
E
A
true.
Dar - ling, I love you.
D
E
A
D
E
To Coda
Mmm.
Mmm.
A
D
E
A

D
E
A
D
E
A
D
E
A
D
E
Play 3 times
A
D
E
D.S. al Coda
CODA
A
D
E
A
Repeat and Fade
Mmm.

YER BLUES

Words and Music by JOHN LENNON
and PAUL McCARTNEY

E7♯9
wan - na die.
wan - na die.
G
If I ain't dead al - read - y,
B
A
G♯m
Gm
F♯m
E7
woo,
girl, you know the rea - son why.
A7
E7
1 B7
2 B7
In the
My

Medium rock shuffle
E7
B7#9
B7#9
moth - er was of the sky. My fa - ther was of the earth. But
ea - gle picks my eye. The worm he licks my bones. I
E7
Tempo I
I am of the u - ni - verse and you know what that's
feel so su - i - ci - dal just like Dy - lan's Mis - ter
E7#9
A7
worth.
Jones.
I'm lone - ly
E7#9
wan - na die.

G
If I ain't dead al - read - y,
B A G#m Gm F#m
woo,
girl, you know the rea - son why.
E7
A7
E7
1 B7
The
2 B7
The
Medium rock shuffle
E7
black clouds crossed my mind,
B7#9
E7
blue mist round my soul.
B7#9
I

E7
feel so_ su-i-ci-dal_ e-ven hate my_ rock and roll._ wan-na
A7
E7
die._ Yeah,_ wan-na die._
G
B7♯5
If I ain't dead al-read-y, woo, girl,_ you know the rea-son
E7
B7
E7♯9
why.

A7
E7#9
G
B7
E7#9
A7

B7
E7#9
A7
E7#9
Tempo One
G
B7#5
E7
D.S. and Fade

YELLOW SUBMARINE

Words and Music by
JOHN LENNON and PAUL McCARTNEY

D
C
G
Em
sailed ___ up to the sun till we
Am
Cmaj7
D
G
found ___ the sea of green. And we
D
C
G
Em
lived ___ be-neath the waves in our
Am
Cmaj7
D
yel - low sub - ma - rine.

Chorus:
G
D
We all live in a yel - low sub - ma - rine,
f
G
yel - low sub - ma - rine, yel - low sub - ma - rine. We all live in a
D
yel - low sub - ma - rine, yel - low sub - ma - rine,
G
D
C
yel - low sub - ma - rine.
And our friends are all on
As we live a life of
mf

G
Em
Am
Cmaj7
board,
man - y more of them
live next
ease,
ev - 'ry one of us
has all we
D
G
D
C
door.
And the band
be - gins to
need.
Sky of blue
and sea of
1
G
play:
3
3
2
G
Em
Am
Cmaj7
D
D.S. and Fade
green in our yel - low sub - ma - rine.

YES IT IS

Words and Music by
JOHN LENNON and PAUL McCARTNEY

A
D
C♯m
E
ba - by wore
and what's more
it's
true,
yes it is.
things we planned,
un - der - stand,
it's
E7
Bm7
true,
yes, it is, it's true,
yes, it is.
I could be hap - py with
F♯m
you by my side,
If I could for - get her,
but
C♯m/B
F♯7
B7
it's my pride,
Yes, it is,
yes, it is
Oh, yes it is,
yeah

E
A
F#m7
B7
Please don't wear red to - night,
E
A
D
B7
this is what I said to - night.
For
E
C#m
A
D
C#m
E
red is the col - or that will make be blue, in spite of you, it's true,
Yes, it is, it's
1
E7
true,
Yes it is.
2
G#
A
E
true,
Yes it is, it's true.

YESTERDAY

Words and Music by JOHN LENNON
and PAUL McCARTNEY

Bb/F F C/E Dm7 G7 Bb F
here to stay, oh I be- lieve in yes - ter- day.
o - ver me, oh yes - ter- day came sud - den- ly.
G/A A7 Dm C Bbmaj7 Dm/A Gm C7
Why she had to go I don't know, she would - n't say.
F G/A A7
I said
Dm C Bbmaj7 Dm/A Gm C F
some - thing wrong, now I long for yes - ter - day.

Em
A7
Yes- ter- day,
love was such an eas - y
Dm
B♭
C
game to play.
Now I need a place to
B♭/F
F
C/E
Dm7
G7
B♭
F
hide a- way,
oh I be- lieve
in yes - ter- day.
F/C
G/B
B♭
F
Mm mm mm mm mm.
rit.

YOU CAN'T DO THAT

Words and Music by
JOHN LENNON and PAUL McCARTNEY

G7
and leave you flat,
Be-cause I've
D7
C7
G7
told you be-fore:
Oh,
you can't
do
that
1 D7
2 G7
B7
Well, it's the
Ev-'ry-bod-y's
green,
Em
Am
B7
Em
'cause I'm the one who won your
love.
But if they'd
seen

B7
Em
Am
you talk - in' that way
they'd
Bm
D
G7
laugh in my face.
So
please lis - ten to me if you
wan - na stay mine,
I
can't help my feel - ings, I'll go
C7
out of my mind.
I'm gon - na
let you down

G7
and leave you flat,
D7
C7
To Coda
Be-cause I've told you be-fore: Oh, you can't do
G7
that.

C7
G7
D7
G7
D.S. al Coda
Ev - 'ry - bod - y's green,
CODA
G7
F
F♯
G
that.

YOU WON'T SEE ME

Words and Music by
JOHN LENNON and PAUL McCARTNEY

A
A7
D
We have lost the time that
I won't want to stay, I
Dm
A
was so hard to find,
don't have much to say,
And I will
But I can
B7
D
A
lose my mind
turn a - way
if you won't see me,
and you won't see me,
D
A
1
You won't see me.
You won't see me.
I don't know

2
A
D6
Dm6
Time af - ter time you re - fuse
A
B7
to ev - en lis - ten.
I would - n't mind.
E7sus
if I knew what I was miss -
E7
A
B7
- ing. Though the days are few, they're filled

D
A
with tears.
And since I
lost you
B7
D
A
it feels
like years.
Yes, it seems
A7
D
Dm
so long
girl, since
you've
been gone,
A
B7
And I just can't
go on
if

1
D
A
D
A
you won't_ see me,
You won't_ see me.
2
D
A
You won't_ see me.
D
A
A
You won't_ see me.
Oo
B7
D
A
Repeat and Fade
la la la
Oo
la la la

YOU KNOW MY NAME
(LOOK UP THE NUMBER)

Words and Music by JOHN LENNON
and PAUL McCARTNEY

A7
D
F♯m
G
A7
num - ber.
You,
you know,
you know my name.
D
F♯m
G
A7
D
You,
you know,
you know my name.
Faster, with a latin beat
Spoken: Good evening and welcome to Slaggers featuring Denis O'Bell.
D
A7
D
A7
Ah, Ringo, let's hear it for Denis. Good evening.

G
F♯+
You know my name,
Bm
E7
Bet-ter look up my num - ber.
G
D
Em
You know my name,
That's right, Look up my num -
A7
D
- ber.
You, you know,

G
A
D
you know my name.
You, you know,
G
A
G
you know my name.
You know my name.
F♯+
Bm
ba ba ba ba ba ba ba ba ba ba,
Look up my num-
E7
G
D
-ber.
You know my name,

Em
A7
That's right, Look up the num - ber. Oh
D
Em
A7
you know, you know, You know my name.
D
Em
A7
G
You know, you know you know my name. Huh huh huh huh. You know my name,
F♯+
F♯
Bm
E7
ba ba ba pum, Look up the num - ber.

G
D
Em
A7
You know my name, Look up the num - ber.
D
Em
A7
D
You - a, you know, you know my name. Ba - by you - a, you know,
Em7
A13
D
Em7
A13
you know my name. You know you know my name,
D
Em7
A13
you know you know my name.
Spoken: Go on Denis, let's hear it for Dennis O'Bell.

D
G
A7
D
You know, you know, you know my name. You know, you know,
G
A7
G
D/F♯
you know my name. Prrr you know my name, Look up the num - ber.
3
Bm
Em
G
D
You know my name, Look up the num - ber. You know,
3
Em
A7
you know my name, Look up the num - ber, You
3

D
G
A7
D
know my num - ber three, you know my num - ber two, you know my num - ber three, you
G
A7
D
G
G♯dim7
know my num - ber four. You know my name, you know my num - ber, too. You
A7
D6
know my name, you know my num - ber. What's up with you? You know my name,
That's right, Yeah.

D
G
A7sus
D
Gmaj9
G
F♯+
Bm
E9
G
D
Em
A7
D
G
A7
D
G
A7
G

F♯+
Bm
E9
G
D
Em7
A7
D
G
A7
D
G
A7
D
G
G♯dim7
D
A7sus
D13

YOU LIKE ME TOO MUCH

Words and Music by
GEORGE HARRISON

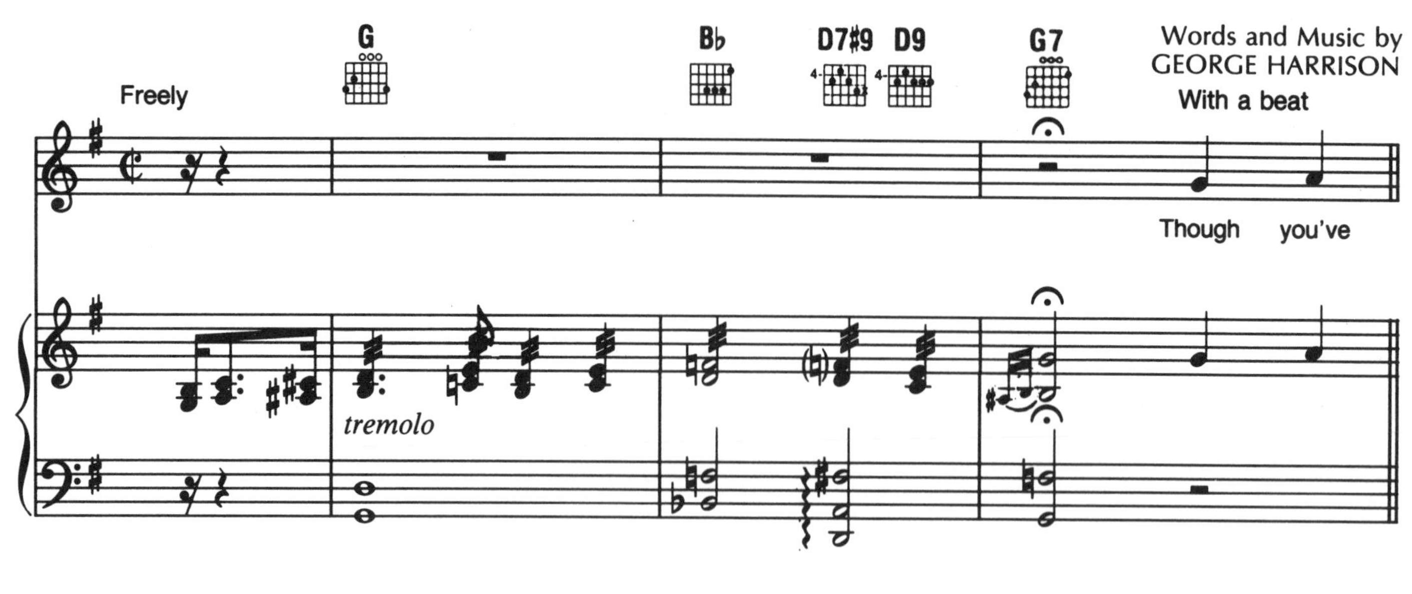

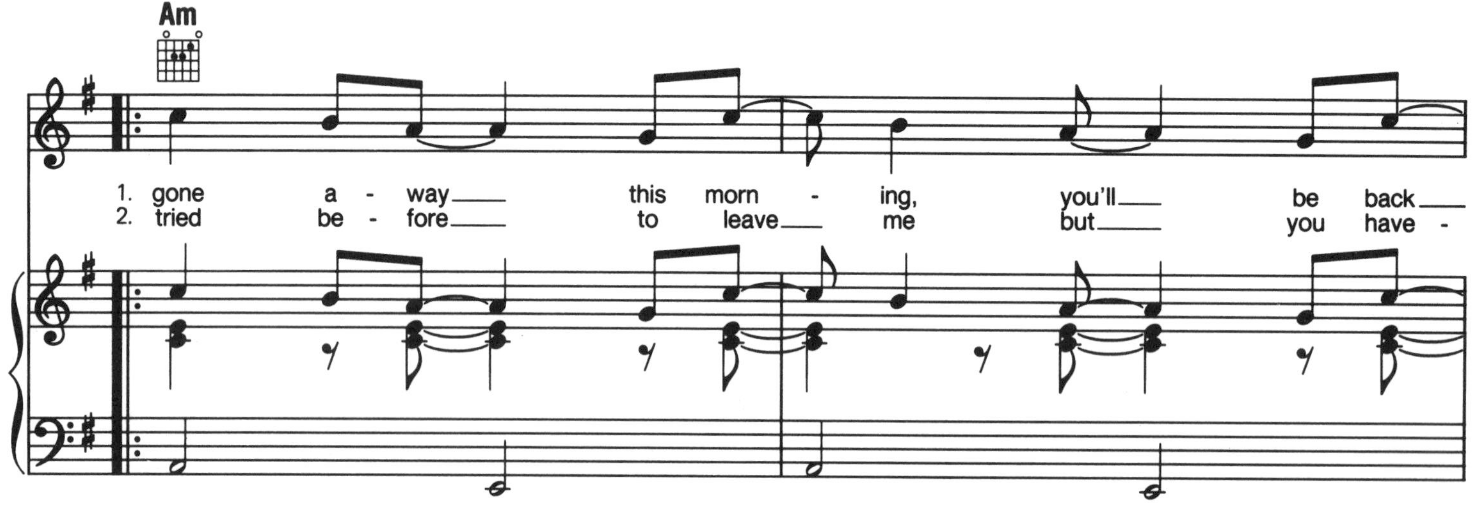

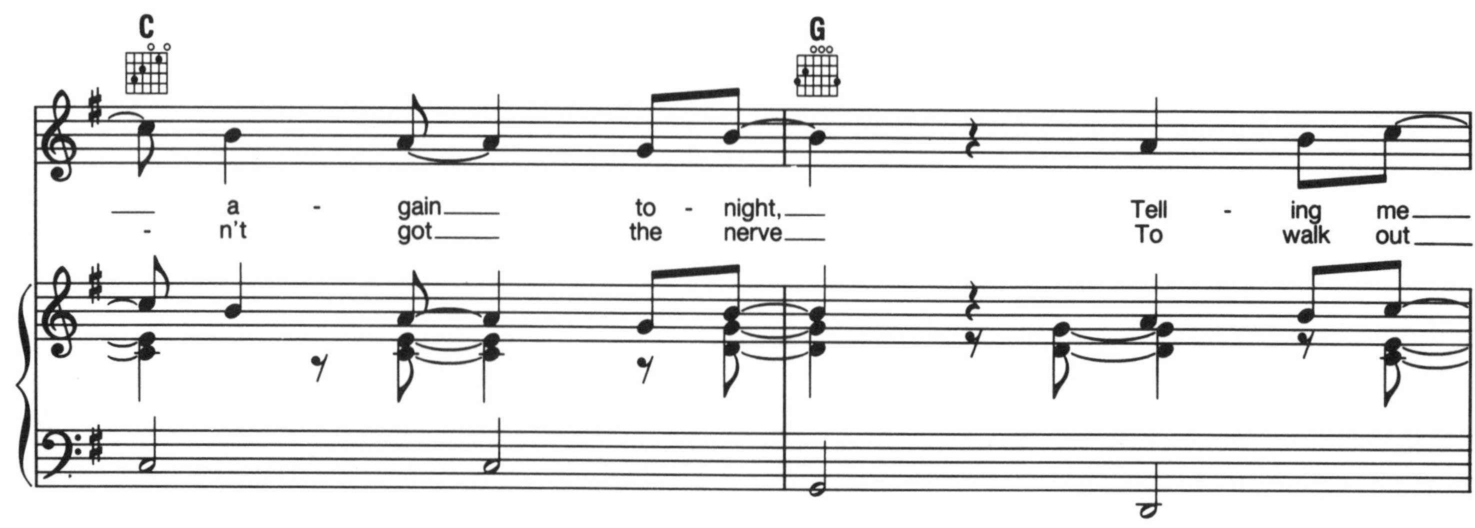

Am
C
there'll be no next time if I just don't treat you right.
and make me lone - ly which is all that I de-serve.
G
Bm
Bm7
You'll nev - er leave me and you know it's true,
You'll nev - er leave me and you know it's true,
D7
G7
'cause you like me too much
'cause you like me too much
C
D
G/D
D
G/D
and I like you.
and I like you.
2. You've

2
D7
Em7
I
real - ly
A7
do.
And it's
Bm7
A
Em7
A7
nice when you be - lieve me.
If you
D7
Am
leave me
I will fol - low you and bring you back

C
G
Am
where you be - long, 'cause I could - n't real - ly stand
C
G
it, I'll ad - mit that I was wrong. I
Bm
Bm7
D7
would - n't let you leave me 'cause it's true,
G7
C
To Coda
'Cause you like me too much and I like you.

D7
G
C
G
D
G7
'Cause you like me too much

C
D7
D.S. al Coda
and I like you.
CODA
D7
G7
'Cause you like me too much
C
D7
G
and I like you.
C
G
C
B♭6
D7♯9
D9
G

YOU NEVER GIVE ME YOUR MONEY

Words and Music by
JOHN LENNON and PAUL McCARTNEY

Bm7-5
E7
Am
1
go - ti - a - tions you break down.
ves - ti - ga - tion I break down.
Twice as fast
2
C
G7
C
E7
Out of col - lege, mon - ey spent,
An - y job - ber got the sack,
Am
C7
F
see no fu - ture, pay no rent,
All the mon - ey's gone,
Mon - day morn - ing, turn - ing back,
Yel - low lor - ry slow,
G7
C
1
no - where to go.
no - where to go.

2
Original tempo
B♭
But oh, that mag - ic feel - ing,
F
C
no - where to go.
B♭
Oh, that mag - ic feel - ing
F
C
no - where to go, no - where to go.
B♭
F
Ah

C
B♭
Ah
F
G
C
D
E♭7
G
C
A7
E♭
C7
3
3

Gb
Eb7
A
F#7
G7
G#7
A7
B
One sweet dream
C
D
E7
A
Pick up the bags and get in the lim - ou - sine
D7
G
D7
G
Soon we'll be a - way from here
Step on the gas and wipe that tear a - way

A
B
Cmaj7
G
One sweet dream came true
A
G
Cmaj7
G
A
to- day came true to- day.
C
G/B
A
C
A
Repeat and Fade
One, two, three, four, five, six, sev-en, All good chil-dren go to heav-en.

YOU REALLY GOT A HOLD ON ME

Words and Music by
WILLIAM "SMOKEY" ROBINSON

A
D
Oh, oh, oh, you treat me bad - ly, I love you
Oh, oh, oh, you do me wrong now, my love is
Oh, oh, oh, I wan - na split now, I just can't

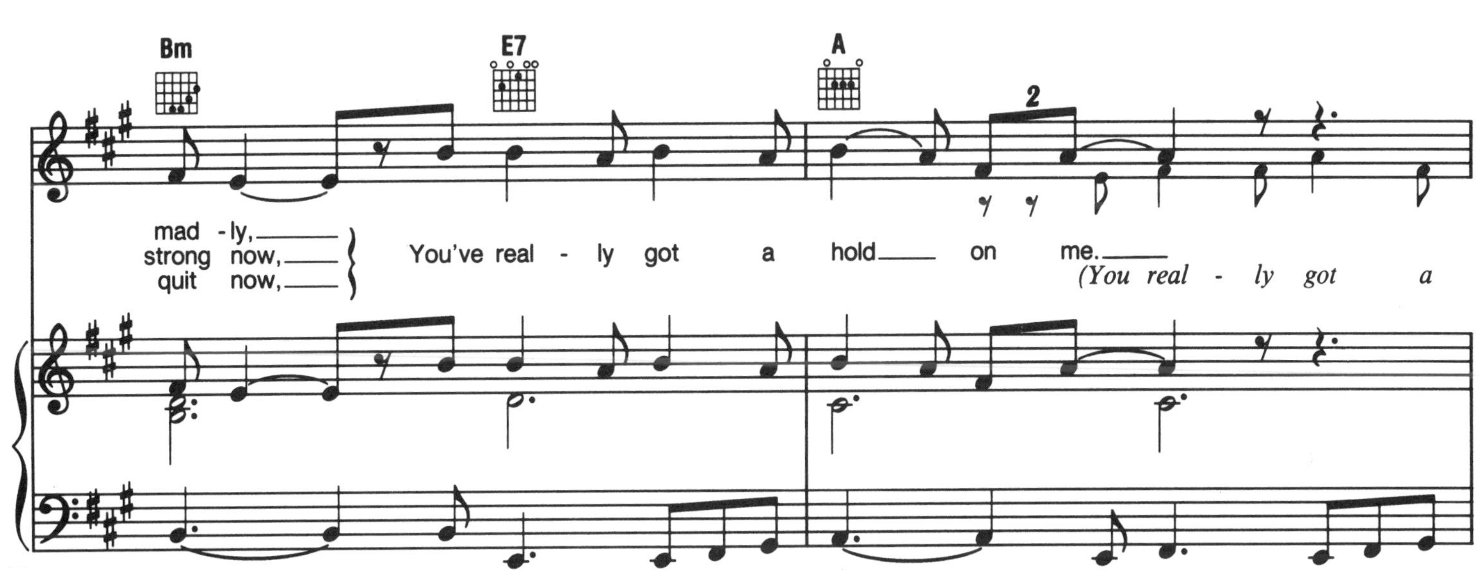
Bm
E7
A
2
mad - ly,
strong now,
quit now,
You've real - ly got a hold on me.
(You real - ly got a

1
F#m
You real - ly got a hold on me. Ba - by,
hold on me.) (You real - ly got a hold on me.)

2,3
F♯m
hold on me.
(You really got a hold on me.)
Baby,
A
A7
D
I love you and all I want you to do is just
A
E7
To Coda
1. hold me, hold me, hold me, hold me.
2. hold me, (please) hold me, (squeeze) hold me, hold me.
A
F♯m
E
A
Tighter

F♯m
E
A
D.S. al Coda
Tight - er!
CODA
A
You real - ly got a hold on me,
(You
real - ly got a hold on me.)
F♯m
You real - ly got a hold on me.
(You
A
real - ly got a hold on me.)

YOU'VE GOT TO HIDE YOUR LOVE AWAY

C
F
C
feel - ing two foot small.
in the state I'm in.
D
G
D
F
G
Ev - 'ry - where peo - ple stare
How could she say to me
C
F
C
each and ev - 'ry day.
"Love will find a way?"
G
D
F
G
C
I can see them laugh at me
Gath - er 'round, all you clowns,
And I hear them
Let me hear you

F
C
D
D/C
say:
say:
D/B
D/A
G
"Hey, you've got to
C
D7sus
D7
hide your love a - way!"
D7(addE)
D7
G
C
"Hey, you've got to hide your love a -

D7sus
D7
D7(addE)
D7
way!"
G
D
F
G
C
(instrumental)
F
C
G
D
F
G
C
F
C
G

YOUR MOTHER SHOULD KNOW

Words and Music by
JOHN LENNON and PAUL McCARTNEY

A7
D7
G7
your moth - er should know,
your moth - er should know.
C
1 E7
2 E
Sing it a - gain:
Broadly
Am
F
Dm/F
G7
C
E7
Sing it a - gain:

Am
Fmaj7
Lift up your hearts and sing me a song that was a
Da da da da da da da da da da da da
A7/E
Dm
hit be - fore your moth - er was born.
da da da da da da da da.
G7
C
C/B
Though she was born a long, long time a - go,
A7
D7
G7
your moth - er should know, your moth - er should know.

C
A7
Your moth - er should know,
D7
G7
1
C
your moth - er should know.
E
2
C
A7
Your moth - er should know,
D7
G7
C
your moth - er should know.

YOU'RE GOING TO LOSE THAT GIRL

Words and Music by
JOHN LENNON and PAUL McCARTNEY

F♯m7
B7
E
change her mind.
find her gone.
And I will take her
'Cause I will treat her
G♯m7
F♯m7
B7
out to- night and I will treat her kind.
right and then you'll be the lone - ly one.
You're gon - na
E
C♯m7
lose that girl.
You're gon - na
F♯m7
1 B7
2 B7
lose that girl.
girl,
You're gon - na

F♯m7
D
G
lose
I'll make a point of
C
G
tak - ing her a - way from you.
Yeah.
The way you treat her,
C
what else can I do?
F
To Coda
E
G♯m7

F♯m7
B7
B7
You're gon - na lose that girl.
lose that girl. You're gon - na
E
C♯m7
F♯m7
lose that girl.
You're gon - na lose that
B7
D.S. al Coda
CODA
E
G♯m7
girl. You're gon-na
If you don't take her out to-night she's gon-na
F♯m7
B7
E
change her mind.
And I will take her

G♯m7
F♯m7
out to - night. and I will treat her kind.
B7
E
C♯m7
You're gon - na lose that girl,
You're gon - na
F♯m7
B7
lose that girl.
You're gon - na
F♯m7
D
A
E
lose, you're gon - na lose that girl.